Taught by Ten

Dr. Ray Guarendi

Taught by Ten
A Psychologist Father Learns from His Ten Children

EWTN Publishing, Inc.
Irondale, Alabama

EWTN Publishing, Inc.
5817 Old Leeds Road, Irondale, AL 35210

Distributed by Sophia Institute Press, Box 5284, Manchester, NH 03108.

paperback ISBN 978-1-68278-261-3

ebook ISBN 978-1-68278-262-0

Library of Congress Control Number: 2022940906

First printing

To Randi, my wife, soulmate, and best friend
and the mother who has taught the children and me so much

Contents

Taught by Ten

Introduction

The voice on the phone was familiar. It belonged to a television producer who had regularly invited me to be a guest. The topic was to be "Navigating the Teen Years."

On the program with me was an educator who was raising two teens. Our give-and-take flowed along smoothly enough until I offered this discipline advice for disrespect: a handwritten apology, the parent setting the length. Eyeing me as if I were a fossil from the Mesozoic era, she pronounced my advice unworkable and challenged, "Do you have any kids?" Eager to certify my paternal status, I replied, "Yes, I have six"—our total at the time. The number did nothing to mollify her. It did, however, supercharge the studio audience, who erupted in hoots and hollers, projecting toward her a collective "In your face!" Or, to unearth lingo from my Mesozoic teen years, "Scorch!"

Unfazed, she fired off, "Are any of them teenagers?"

"No, not yet."

Smugly she sat back, as the gallery pivoted its group "Gotcha" at me.

She and they were voicing the same faulty assumption: You can't give good advice to another unless you've lived her experience yourself. You must walk, if not a mile, at least a while in her

3

shoes. Only then can you rightfully claim to know what you're talking about.

During graduate school, I conducted group therapy at a Veteran's Administration hospital. One member of the group had served time in prison. Within the first minutes of the first session, he scowled at me, hurling a salvo of questions. "How old are you?" Twenty-four. I was tempted to add, "But I'll be twenty-five in a few months." "You ever been in jail?" No, not yet anyway. "Then what are you going to tell me?"

Momentarily broadsided, I regrouped enough to answer, "Because I've never been in jail, maybe I can tell you a few things about living better out of jail." Judging by his stony stare, my clever riposte did little to satisfy him.

With certainty, I can assert that I am not a woman. Yet more than half of those who seek my guidance are female. Neither am I a troubled teen, an octogenarian, or an atheist. I have no history of legal troubles, alcohol or drug abuse, violence, or mental illness. My wife says I could personally relate well to eleven-year-olds, though.

"You can't talk it until you've walked it." Taken to its illogical extreme, this would limit my practice to white males who are fathers and who've been married to the same woman for thirty-plus years. My range of clients would be pretty slim.

I wrote my first book before I had children—in fact, before I was married. Because parents routinely told me of their insecurities, undue guilt, and wobbly authority, I titled it *You're a Better Parent Than You Think!* I mean, who buys parenting books other than those wanting to be better parents?

With a book to my name, I still heard, "Do you have any children?" No, but I was a child myself once.

The question more often comes from those who don't like what they're hearing. Seldom does someone object to guidance that confirms how he is already doing things, no matter how little the experience of the one giving it.

I grew up as a psychologist by listening to countless parents and kids, absorbing their experiences—good and bad. If I haven't learned over all these years, I haven't been paying attention.

I grew up as a parent by living with ten children. If I haven't learned over all those kids, I haven't been paying attention. The all day, every day of raising children forges and forces insights. It allows one to say, "I've walked the talk." Personal experience can soften words that may be hard for some to hear.

A lesson that wove its way through many lessons for me is: Relax and laugh more. The antics, impulses, and nuttiness that come so naturally to kids could be the stuff of television sitcoms. Oh wait, it is.

I shed some of my early bent to overanalyze. I learned to surf the crests and troughs of the child-rearing waves until settling, often anyway, in smoother waters.

As one mother captured it, "Parenting is far too important to be taken too seriously."

Lesson 1

God's Plans Are Better Than Ours

Flashbulb memory—an experience so emotionally charged that it sears itself into one's mind. It frames a vivid mental picture of the minutiae of the moment. For those older, one such memory might be their when and where upon first hearing of President Kennedy's assassination. For those younger, it might be watching Neil Armstrong's moon walk. Still younger, watching Michael Jackson's moonwalk.

A personal flashbulb memory was fixed the day my wife, Randi, and I together absorbed the results of my fertility tests. We sat side by side in a brown Queen Anne chair in front of our living-room window on a winter afternoon. The low-lying sun brightened the room but not our moods. Randi's eyes moistened as I shared my diagnosis, along with the doctor's verdict: "If you conceive, head for television to talk about your miracle." While sounding brusque, he didn't mean to be. I had asked for the blunt reality. As it turned out, we did get a miracle of sorts. And I have talked about it on television.

Couples trying to conceive but without success hear well-meaning words: "You might just need more time"; "If you can relax, nature can cooperate"; "We have friends who, right in the middle of their adoption plans, got pregnant."

Taught by Ten

True enough, sometimes. Not for us, though. My condition: Sertoli single-cell syndrome, a type of congenital—present from birth—male infertility. My grandmother said that at least it sounded Italian. I toyed with suing my mother, but my attorney said the statute of limitations had probably run out. So I let Mom off with a stern warning: "This better not happen again."

Our family prospects appeared to have smacked headlong into a wall, and a high one at that, as Randi had always hoped to be a mom of a bunch.

As we sat on that Queen Anne chair, we agreed, "Let's try to adopt." Easier contemplated than completed, we knew. Even thirty-plus years ago, adoption was fast becoming a longer, more iffy quest. Our hope was to adopt one child, maybe two. Three was a distant dream. God had another number in mind.

Why adopt?

Simple answer: Randi told me to.

Simpler answer: Tax benefits. Adopt in December, and you still can claim the deduction for the whole year. Our daughter Hannah came to us on December 6. That year, I plopped a little extra in her piggy bank.

Simplest answer: We wanted a family.

The simplest answer is the real answer: We wanted a family, though we had no clue about its final size. On my wedding day, had someone predicted, "You will have ten children," I would have shown her my driver's license: "I think you're mistaking me for someone in the bridal party."

Our first unsteady adoption steps included composing a one-page "personal profile" letter to be sent to several hundred attorneys. Stacked in a dining room corner, the pile awaited send-off until Randi finished her master's thesis.

Hearing of our missive mountain, Randi's mom came to us determined: "Let's mail those letters."

"I'll be done with school in a few weeks," countered Randi. "Then we can send them."

"No, Randi, let's do it today." Mom's insistence was completely out of character for a woman who gave her opinion only when asked—and only when in writing. (I loved her!) So out went the letters, heading in all directions.

No more than a few days later, an attorney who had never arranged an adoption and who was about to retire called. A colleague had walked into his office, asking, "Do you know anyone who would like to adopt a baby?" A young woman had just entered their building after exiting a bus she had taken to visit a nearby hospital for a pregnancy check-up.

Foraging in his wastebasket, where he had summarily dropped our letter that morning, the lawyer answered, "I think so." The trash hadn't yet been collected.

His call came on Ash Wednesday.

On the evening before our first meeting, while I was playing basketball, another player's finger found my eye, shattering my contact lens and leading to a quick trip to the emergency room. Sporting a two-inch-square eye patch, I shuffled into our house. After hearing that my eye would be all right, Randi had her own headache: "What about our appointment tomorrow?" Anxious to show ourselves a stable married couple, she worried how the attorney might react to her pirate-patched husband. Winking with my good eye, I offered to find a stand-in, for our first meeting anyway. Randi considered that but figured we probably couldn't locate one on such short notice. So, to compensate for my face, I promised to put my best foot forward.

Fortunately, the attorney liked basketball. Andrew was born to us several weeks later on Randi's father's birthday.

The good news: From start to finish, our first adoption spanned a few months, unlike a wait that could stretch into years. The bad news: The odds against adopting a second time had jumped. Birth mothers lean toward childless couples, preferring their babies to be a family's first. Even so, we listed our names with an adoption agency.

A year and a half later, the agency contacted us. They were serving a birth mother who, as a child, had always wanted but never had a big brother. Wanting a big brother for her baby girl, she heard of Andrew, who, at a year and a half, was ready for the role.

One boy, one girl—the "ideal" American family. Any more children, and we'd be confronting a culture that censures marrieds with any more than two children, the new and approved number. Defying society, we told the agency, "Please consider us for any child who might be harder to place."

Two years later, the call came. "Are you still wanting to adopt?"

"Absolutely!" Randi nearly shouted.

Because I wasn't home, they asked, "Do you need to talk to Ray first?"

"No."

As I said, the simple answer: "Randi told me to." But I did agree.

Moving from two kids to three, to use a football analogy, is like moving from a man-to-man defense to a zone defense. The little people outnumber the big people. They are capable of more moves than we have countermoves.

We assumed our adoption days were likely over. At a high school reunion, however, a former classmate told us of an attorney who specialized in placement across race. Thirty years ago, the adoption world was nearly unanimous: Openness to a child of any race or to one with "special needs" (an umbrella term from mild to severe) would not only shorten the wait but would broaden the options.

Back then, I asked a placement specialist, "How long would we wait to adopt a child of a race different from ours?" She wryly answered, "What are you doing tomorrow?"

Not long after listing our names with the attorney, she told us about a birth mother wanting to place her bi-racial son with a psychologist. She worried that her own struggles with alcohol might pass genetically to him. Samuel is now twenty-eight, with no such struggles. Who would have thought the letters after my name would spell another child for us?

Sam was not developing normally in the womb. Two weeks before his due date, he weighed just four pounds. Testing was conducted, with the tentative diagnosis being "Corpus callosum agenesis," a potentially serious brain malformation. The worst outcome would require round-the-clock skilled care.

How many voices, I wonder, had pushed Sam's thirty-five-year-old birth mother toward aborting her baby? Instead, she carried him to birth, premature but healthy. The ultrasound test was completely inaccurate.

A number of our children were at high risk for abortion. Consequently, we stressed to them their birth mothers' love in giving them not only a family but life itself.

All was quiet on the home front—in numbers, not decibels—until a year later. At a training meeting, a social worker handed me a picture of twins in foster care awaiting a permanent home. When Randi saw their photo, she placed it on the refrigerator—most families' domestic gallery of people portraits. We all prayed that the twins would find a quiet, peaceful home, or barring that, ours!

We were open to adding, but it was a nervous open. With children ages five, four, two, and baby, adding two more preschoolers to the mix would be like throwing "fizzies" into an already carbonated drink.

Hearing nothing for months, we assumed the kids had long since been adopted. Then came a phone call: "Dr. and Mrs. Guarendi, you are the family of choice." Initially I thought, "Family of choice for what? A car? a TV? a trip to Disneyworld?" Then I heard: "As a family for Jonathan and Joanna."

In fact, we were not the family of first choice or even the second. Because we already had four young children, the agency was looking toward smaller families. Neither of the first two, however, ultimately pursued the adoption. We were, you could say, a home by default. Which was fine by us.

Why the families exited, we didn't know, but we had some sense after coming face-to-face with Jon's unbridled unruliness. Among his other, to use shrink talk, nonverbal manifestations of frustration, he punched me in the face—at his age, he really couldn't hit that hard—grabbed Randi by the throat, and launched serial displays of temper fireworks.

After one particularly raucous visit, Randi expressed a moment of misgiving, "Should we rethink this? Is the tax deduction really that big?" I corrected, "Not one, but two tax deductions, plus the child credits." Okay, maybe our dialogue has since been a bit embellished. Still, we were nervous over how the twins' habits might affect our other kids—and us.

It didn't take all that long to find out. Sarah, age three, began to bite this newcomer Joanna. In turn, Joanna ran to tattle the instant Sarah's teeth made their mark. Sarah had never been a biter. She used her mouth to talk us numb, so we suspected that Joanna was a sly provocateur. As yet, Hannah, their older sibling, had not assumed her birthright duty to provide us with written reports on each sibling's misconduct.

Our strategy to clamp down on Sarah's biting can't be found in any parenting book except this one. "Joanna, if Sarah bites you, you both will stand in the corner." Joanna's stunned look declared, "What kind of justice is that?" After several dual corner stays, though, Sarah kept her teeth in her mouth, and Joanna kept her tattle in hers.

How long for our new discipline normal to return to our old discipline normal? Months. More later on the power of perseverance.

Like a roller-coaster ride, Jonathan and Joanna's adoption came complete with upside-down twists and turns. A few days after their arrival, during a presentation to a parent group, I mentioned their names. Afterward, a woman approached me, "I thought you might want to see this." Pictured on the local paper's front page, in obvious distress, were the former foster parents. The article's tone was plain: Two children were taken from them and given to "strangers."

This marked the first hill of the coaster, which lasted several weeks. Meeting with agency personnel, we were assured that an extensive staff meeting had unanimously decided that, in the "children's best interests"—to use legal jargon—they were to be placed in our home.

In turn, we committed to stay the adoption course as long as the agency's commitment to us remained solid. Other considerations also influenced us. One, the foster parents were a generation older than we were, and one of them was in fragile health. Would both be present for the children's full childhood? And two, having lost his son at age nineteen, the foster father blamed God, Who he wasn't sure even existed. Would the kids be raised in a home that had rejected God?

Thinking things settling, we were stunned to hear from the agency's board: "We're reconsidering our position." Given that they had just been served with a multimillion-dollar lawsuit, their timing did seem suspicious. The suit's main claim was that to move the children now would set in motion long-term attachment deficits.

The unfolding story titillated local radio and television. It was unsettling for us to hear nightly, "Tonight on Channel N., the latest update on the N. twins." Among the many unfounded speculations: The children were payment to an unidentified person for staff training.

Hoping the facts would come to light, we initially refrained from defending ourselves. After days of slanted coverage, however, I contacted a fair-minded radio personality before he went on air, sharing with him the broader story. Surprised, he felt he had been badly misled. From that day, the juggernaut began to lose momentum.

Before a final ruling, several board members asked to meet with us. In preparation, I researched several hundred papers on attachment. There was as yet no Internet to speed my quest. The finding: Attachment struggles are most likely to arise when a child has had multiple disrupted living situations. From a foster to an adoptive home is not a risky emotional move.

After the meeting, one board member remarked, "You really did your homework." Yes, I did. In the end, the agency settled out of court for a miniscule fraction of the original lawsuit.

Years later, I received an apologetic phone call from the foster dad acknowledging that the best decision had been made. He also told me that his wife had passed away some years prior. A few years later, so did he. Both died while the children were still minors.

We had bumped our heads on our family ceiling, or so it felt. Three more years passed, and Randi, an Evangelical Christian, was inching toward the Catholic Church. Praying at our local Sancta Clara Monastery, where Mother Angelica, foundress of the Catholic network EWTN, was the former superior, she asked, "Lord, if you have a child for us, show us." No longer were we actively looking.

The next morning, we heard from the attorney who had arranged Sam's adoption: "I have a baby boy, born two months premature and in the neonatal intensive care unit [NICU]. Are you interested?" If we weren't, the attorney had one other potential family several states away.

Only hours earlier, Randi had prayed that if God were to give, we would accept. The timing did seem a little too providential.

Peter was born at a little over three pounds. He spent his first month in the NICU with wires and tubes entering and leaving his tiny body. Because he was so developmentally delicate, it was weeks before we could take him home.

During his preschool years, Pete and I would meet my parents for breakfast. I don't recall what my mother said one day to get his five-year-old mind musing, but as we were driving away from the restaurant, Pete began his inquisition.

"Dad, you were in Grandma's belly when you were a really little baby, weren't you?"

"Yes, Petey, I was."

"Was I in Mommy's belly?"

Oh boy, here we go. And I'm in the car, without my wife. Well, I guess now's as good a time as any to talk.

"No, Peter, you weren't. You were in another mommy's belly."

Silence, he was processing. Maybe he would process long enough for me to get home and find Randi. No chance.

"How did I get in there?"

Great. I just dodged the adoption talk only to face the facts-of-life talk. As a shrink, I'm trained: When in doubt, seek clarification.

"What do you mean, Pete?"

"You know, who put me in there?"

An accurate answer can involve God, while ducking unwanted specifics.

"God put you in there."

"How did He do that?"

"What do you mean, Pete?"

I wholeheartedly advise the "What do you mean?" strategy for a range of parent-child discourses.

"I mean, did He throw me down in there, or did He just lay me in there?"

I might take it home after all. Pete was just asking boy-type questions.

"Well, Pete, that's easy. He just laid you in there."

Dead silence. Discussion closed. Peter was satisfied—for one traffic light. Then came his grand finale. "Why didn't she keep me?"

I didn't have my cell phone to call Randi, so it looked as if I was on my own.

"Petey, she wanted you to have a mommy and a daddy, and she didn't have a daddy for you. So she looked for a mommy and a daddy. God knew you needed a daddy, and He also knew I needed a Petey, so He put us together."

Deafening silence, but this time with an "I get it" nod. Seconds later, Pete noticed a tractor trailer hauling cows, and it captured his curiosity. "Daddy, why do cows stink so bad?" By the time we reached home, I was feeling pretty full of myself. I had handled the whole interchange without one time falling back on, "I think you need to ask Mom about this."

I am white; Pete is black. While he didn't know about the birds and bees, he did know his colors. But until that day, he never chased their implications.

Fast-forward twenty years. Pete is a sturdy young man, in body and spirit.

In the late 1990s, changes in federal laws opened for adoption a large number of children in a nearby county. Most of the kids had been placed when a friend from a state agency alerted us that a three-year-old boy was still waiting for a home. I was skittish, but Randi said, "If not us, who?" We had a good marriage, the resources, and the kids voted yes. During the interview, we were informed, "James has a half sister also ready for adoption." Something told me they were timing that revelation for just the right moment.

Restaurants attract patrons with an "Order one meal, get the second meal free." Was this the agency's version of that? Well, just as the freebie meal come-on works, so, too, did the agency's. Mary, age two, joined James.

Nine kids was testing our load limit. We were ready to call it quits. Two years later, a friend called me: "My son's girlfriend is pregnant, and they want to place the baby, but they want a private adoption. Can you help them find a couple?"

This young mother was nearing the end of her pregnancy, so our search was urgent. We found a family who, only days before the birth, had to decline for personal reasons. To our surprise, the birth mother asked us to be her baby's parents. This made Elizabeth an "unplanned adoption." We hadn't been practicing "safe phone."

Before kids, we never looked ahead: "What say we go for ten kids? That's a nice metric number. We'll have two basketball teams or a baseball team with one sub." Adoption just seemed to unfold naturally, though we now believe it unfolded by an unseen hand. Actually, each addition expanded the family by an ever smaller percentage. From one to two, the gain was 100 percent, from two to three, 50 percent. Nine to ten, a meager 11 percent. Numerically speaking, it got easier.

Given our ages at marriage and assuming no complications, conceivably—no pun intended—we might have birthed three, at the most four, children. God gave us triple that number. He picked up the pieces of what once looked like broken parenthood and reassembled them into a much fuller picture.

God knows us infinitely better than we know ourselves. He knows our limits better than we do. He may hand us more than we bargained for, but He hands us the better part of the bargain.

When the kids were small, mothers would sometimes ask Randi, "How do you do it? I'm frustrated with my two." Randi's answer, "More children don't make you a worse parent. They make you a better one."

Judgments are more confident, discipline more sure. You ruffle more slowly. Less confuses you. Less throws you off child-rearing balance. If the first three children tried the same stunt, the fourth doesn't rattle you with it. As my son Peter would say, you learn how kids roll.

Our diverse personalities at home helped my career. As a parent talked of some unsettling piece of kid conduct, I could sometimes confess, "I remember when one of my kids did that." Their look said, "Really?" That the shrink's kid acted much like theirs made them feel less inept. Or maybe it made me look more inept.

Glad to be of help.

Lesson 2

We Don't Know What God Knows

Our first child's birth mother asked that we be at the hospital for his birth. She wished for Randi, his life mother, to be the first to hold him. It was a young teen's beautiful gesture to two people who might never again have that moment.

With us during the hours before the birth was a nurse friend delivering enthusiastic updates. At last, she announced, but soberly, "He's here." I thought, "'He's here'? That's it? After all this excited buildup?" She added, "The doctor will be in to talk to you." Those are scary words. It would be a long, unsettled wait. That is not how we anticipated our first steps into parenthood.

Andrew was born with a complex cleft of the lip and palate. Prior to modern surgery, children with such conditions were social outcasts, throwaways. In some places in the world, they still are. They could never speak or eat normally and were thought mentally impaired. Indeed, not all that long ago in our own society, they were targeted for abortion.

Andrew would need multiple surgeries as a baby and as a young child, with a last one coming at age twenty-six. How would it all go—for him and for us? Would we be sturdy, cool-headed companions? Or would we struggle to keep our emotions stable for his sake? In time, we came to understand better what parents of children with special needs much more involved than Andrew's understand. You stand stronger because you love, because your child needs you to. With God's grace as your brace, you walk through what comes, with a reservoir of resolve.

At age two, Andrew was having blood drawn for his fourth surgery. Finding a visible vein on a two-year-old is like finding a four-leaf clover in a patch of three-leafers. As the veteran nurse probed repeatedly for a cooperative vein, Andrew's little body twisted and torqued in resistance. Keeping him still was proving futile. Randi left the room in tears.

"Can I hold him for you?" I asked the nurse. She agreed, so I held Andrew down tightly. Immediately, he turned toward me with a look of betrayal, as if to plead, "Daddy, why are you helping them hurt me?" I thought, "Andrew, if you only knew what I know."

As I've woven my way through some unforeseen pains and strains of parenthood, I've had to wonder, "Is God thinking, 'Ray, if you only knew what I know.'" He sees the full picture, from inception to finish. I see, at most, bits and pieces at a time.

When Andrew was born, after a week at the hospital learning the ins and outs of his care, he and Randi and I were on an elevator, heading home. Andrew was asleep, his face covered by his infant carrier. A man entered and smiled at this mom with her newborn. "Can I see your baby?" Randi felt a protective twinge, unsure what his reflexive reaction might be upon seeing a less than perfectly formed face. As she pulled back the carrier's blanket, he declared, without missing a microbeat, "He's absolutely beautiful." On the main floor, he exited the elevator ahead of us. As we exited, Randi took a quick look in both directions. There was no sign of him.

People talk of being visited by heavenly messengers. Whether or not this man was one, I don't know. I do know he was a messenger.

Thirty-four years later, Andrew is a faith-filled father and holds an advanced degree in engineering. So much for the archaic idea that cleft features equal intellectual poverty. Predicting what long-off future days hold is perfected by God alone. We simply can't foresee or know what He knows.

Our twins contracted hepatitis C in the womb. It was discovered at age sixteen. At the time, the best treatment, a form of chemotherapy, was about 50 percent effective. After a year-long regimen, neither twin was cured. The virus stubbornly survived. Both teens were left with a chronic, likely life-shortening illness. Ten years later, much more potent antivirals emerged, curing both young adults.

Our middle son enlisted in the army at age twenty-one. A few years into his tour, he was diagnosed with cancer. During his treatment and surgery, he hid his diagnosis from us, later confiding, "I didn't want to worry you guys." Son, we could have prayed while we worried. He remains cancer free.

Some of our children were exposed to alcohol and drugs in the womb, a daughter most heavily so. Consequently, childhood for her was a turbulent journey, ultimately leading to a string of group homes in her late teens and early twenties. Her life has been a tragic story clustered with self-destructive decisions.

"Wouldn't you have wanted to know what the future held for your family?" Definitely not. Knowing beforehand what distress could lie somewhere beyond the horizon can only shatter serenity in one's present.

No surprise, but Andrew developed a fear of needles. Shortly before kindergarten, he found out he would have to have a "shot," something he fretted about off and on for weeks. At age nineteen, he was diagnosed with type 1 diabetes, requiring several needle jabs per day. He conquered his fear of needles because he had to.

It's basic psychology: We are not good at predicting how we will react when faced with crises. Countless parents recount for me circumstances they never believed they could endure, let alone overcome. All along the way, they underestimated the depth of their emotional reserves.

Few relationships embody unconditional love like that of a parent for a child. Love like no other begets strength of spirit like no other.

Lesson 3

Respect the Power of Temperament

"Children twelve and under eat free." So tempt restaurants. Words that belie the aphorism "There's no such thing as a free lunch." We ate plenty of free lunches. Over the years, I estimate that "Children twelve and under eat free" probably saved me a few thousand dollars.

Two free kids per adult was the standard ratio. We stumbled upon one place, though, that enticed: "Two adult orders and all children twelve and under eat gratis." We had struck menu gold.

Every Sunday, we'd troop in with all our kids under thirteen. The bill totaled less than fifteen bucks. My mother, raised during the Depression of the 1930s, seldom entered any restaurant without her discount coupons. She was so proud of us.

One Sunday, the meal deal was gone. "What happened?" I asked the manager. "You did," he replied. We had broken the bank. The place no longer had the appetite to feed so many for so little. Oh well, we had a good run.

We took to foraging for food. We ate by St. Paul's words to the Corinthians: "I buffet my body" (see 1 Cor. 9:27). His was good counsel, as our adolescent boys ate anything that didn't eat them first.

One place featured a costumed bee circling the tables, dropping off sweets—as if the hundred-plus food options weren't enough.

When Mr. Bee hovered over to our table, James, age four, cried and cringed behind his mother. Peter, age three, with an unspoken "Buzz off," popped him straight in his plastic nose. Consequently, no treat. That stung him.

Did anything in our parenting shape James's anxious recoil? Not that we could see. How about Peter's reflexive "Swing first and ask questions later"? Again, nope. Both boys acted in accord with their personalities, prompting us to act in accord with ours: James was comforted; Pete was disciplined.

Was Pete "strong-willed"? The better word would be "intense." From the get-go, he was wired to run face first fast at life.

Little kids approach bedtime from two directions—bliss or bedlam. Bedlam would have directed our nights were we not definite: Battling bedtime was asking for consequences, immediately or at first light tomorrow. Lack of sleep makes kids cranky. It makes parents even more cranky.

One child was the slowest to make bedtime bliss time. Three guesses who, and the first two don't count. One evening, it all came pouring out. From the top of the stairs, we heard a self-satisfied cackle, as if to dare, "No bed made can hold me." Leaping from his crib and sneaking into the bathroom, Pete grabbed his potty-chair bowl, which we had neglected to empty, and to remind us, summarily dumped its liquid contents down several steps. It was his "number one" bed-defying move.

Tired of corraling Pete at bedtime, Randi bought an umbrella shaped net to fit over his crib. Apparently, it was an in-demand item, as it had to be backordered. The net shrank my self-image as a shrink. After all, I'm supposed to know how to make nighttime nice time.

The net stilled the night for a few weeks. Then a split started to form in its tough nylon webbing. What, or more likely, who, was opening the escape hatch? Suspecting who, but with no visual proof, one night I stood silently watching outside Pete's room as he lay still with eyes closed. After a few minutes, scanning for grown-ups, he felt under his mattress for a stashed plastic knife, pilfered from the older kids' toy kitchen. Reaching up, he commenced sawing away at that confining net. To our knowledge, Pete had never seen any TV prison-escape scenes. His mind just naturally hatched the plot.

Fast-forward twenty-four years. Pete is still intense but is a young man who intently talks faith and philosophy with his old dad. And he no longer needs a net to stay in bed. We presented it to him when he moved out.

Our first two children were Andrew and Hannah. As we had no need for a minivan yet, a paneled station wagon was our idea of trav-eling chic. One trip, Andrew, age four, started to nag for ice cream.

"No, buddy, we're heading home."

In an impulsive "Let's see if I can add some kick to my demand," Andrew swung his feet against the back of my driver's seat, a rather feeble display of pique.

"Andrew, you're in the corner when we get home."

"Why, Daddy?"

"Because that's a fit."

Dripping with disdain, his two-year-old sister corrected me, "That's not a fit." Her meaning: "Don't applaud that amateur. He's not in my league." Indeed, Hannah had earned an early nick-name—Miss Fitsky.

Andrew was wired the polar opposite of intense. When he was a toddler and his mother took from him some off-limits item, his demeanor said, "If you want it, here. I can find other amusement." When Randi took anything from toddler Hannah, she instantly flared with a "How dare you! Give it back. Now!"

Taught by Ten

Andrew's nature lulled us to sleep. Hannah's woke us up. We thought him typical, her tough. In fact, he was easy; she was typical. More later on shell-shocked second-child syndrome.

For a long time, psychology elevated nurture (one's experiences) above nature (one's inborn personality). In the nature-versus-nurture competition, nurture was the unquestioned victor. Employ proper, psychologically savvy child-rearing, and a parent could pretty much guarantee the desired outcome.

Reality tests all theories. And reality always wins. Nature is earning its due. It is who a child is at her core that every parent acts toward and reacts to. Just as no two parents are alike in patience, perseverance, stamina, judgment, affection, and on and on, no two children are alike in intellect, activity, drive, impulsiveness, fretfulness, and on and on.

Little Chastity enters the world with "Hello, Mother. I've been waiting months to meet you. Should I sleep through the first night home or the second? And please forgive me, but I won't be able to give you much help around the house until I'm at least two years old."

Spike thunders into the delivery room seeking a celebratory cigar and scaring the doctor into giving you her private phone number.

Some of our children tempted us to believe we were God's gift to parenthood. After a few well-timed pieces of discipline, they didn't misbehave for days, leaving mints and love notes on our pillows every night. Okay, small exaggeration. They couldn't write yet. They drew pictures.

Others of our children squirreled food and water away in every corner in case their visits there came too close together or lasted too long.

If you're raising a Spike or a Spikette, and your friend a Chastity or an Oxford, you can be discipline twins—same words, tone, consequences, consistency. After three months, your friend will crow, "I cured the problem eleven weeks ago," and you'll confess, "I don't think he's done it for the past hour, but he is asleep."

Five boys and five girls—our family blend. And that blend showed us every day something society downplays and, however possible, pushes to erase—innate differences between the sexes. The brain, however, pushes back, refusing to surrender to society's opinions. Neither do God, human history, and research surrender.

For example, little boys tend to be more active and hard-charging than little girls. They engage their surroundings more frenetically. Little girls tend to be more verbal. They talk earlier, they talk better—they talk longer. Parents who believe the culture's fallacies are regularly taught otherwise by their children.

After his first day in kindergarten, I asked Andrew, "How was school today?" Good. Counseling 101: Keep asking open-ended questions. "What did you do?" Not much. "You had to do something." We did. "What was that?" Stuff.

When open-ended fails, get specific. "What is the name of the lady who stands in front of your class?" "I'm not sure she told anybody, Dad. Joshua says his is called 'teacher.' I'll ask her if they're related."

After her first day in kindergarten, I asked Hannah, "How was school today, Hannie?" "Well, Daddy, my teacher's name is Mrs. Schmidts—S-c-h-m-i-d-t-s. She has three children: Jessica, Jason, and Ashley. I know their birthdays, middle names, and favorite colors. I'll tell you those in a minute. We did twelve activities today, thirteen if you count lunch. The pumpkin-cutting activity we started at 8:07. I don't think it should have been first, but I didn't say anything to Mrs. Schmidts about it. Maybe tomorrow I will. Tara said she would be my forever friend until Friday.

"Mrs. Schmidts has a little brown mark right behind her left ear. You can't really see it unless she goes over to the shelf by the window and bends down to get something. I don't think she knows it's there, so I raised my hand to tell her. At first, she didn't call on me, so I kept my hand up until she did. Wait, there's more!"

They both had the same teacher.

All right, maybe some exaggeration. The differences, though, while not characterizing every boy and girl, shows itself often enough.

After thirty-plus years of parenting, my wife and I have seen how our children's innate personalities are inextricably tied to so much—how they mature, how they react to discipline, how they relate to others, how they see the world, how they embrace the Faith. The power of temperament reveals itself one child at a time, one day at a time, sometimes one minute at a time.

One mother summed it up: "You're not as bad a parent as your toughest child. And you're not as good a parent as your easiest child."

Lesson 4

Lose the Label

"Strong-willed": a leading label for children these days. Only "boy" and "girl" outrank it. "Strong-willed" is shorthand for a host of descriptions. "He is so oppositional." "She is very stubborn." "He's quite the challenge." "She has a mind of her own." "He's overly defiant." "She is eight going on eighteen." "He's a difficult child." Is "difficult child" redundant?

Consider a newborn. He enters the world with a demanding wail: "Meet my needs!" He wants what he wants, immediately or sooner, expecting that the entire universe exists to provide it. His will is strong all right and is thoroughly self-concerned. He needs years, along with loads of grown-up help, to move beyond "me first."

This picture is neither unduly negative nor overstated. It is the human condition at its outset. It is all of us way back when.

"Strong-willed" implies a will outside the bounds of "normal." If Will were a more typical kid, he'd supposedly be more agreeable to guidance. He'd be less his way and more your way.

The most cooperative child still doesn't see parenthood through a parent's eyes, not consistently anyway. Would even the sweetest Angela concede, "Mom, I'm sorry I had to be almost six years old before I learned that you always know better than I do. Please, don't ever be slow to discipline me. And if you forget, I'll remind you." Now this is not a normal child.

Christians should be slowest to christen a child "strong-willed," as we confess Original Sin, the inward bent toward the self. G. K. Chesterton, a clear-eyed social commentator, observed that the Christian teaching on Original Sin is one with overwhelming real-life evidence. Just watch the news for an hour.

My mother-in-law, who raised five children, once stated, "I don't remember my friends and me talking about how willful our kids were, as so many young parents do nowadays." Her recollection would seem to speak for many of her generation.

Who or what is rocketing "strong-willed" to the peak of parents' vocabulary? The "what" is rapid cultural decay. Society's reigning standards are swirling ever faster down the drain, hostile to anyone striving to raise a morally mature child. This makes standing strong as a parent ever more challenging. Still, this doesn't explain why so many little ones, as yet mostly cocooned from the culture's tentacles, are getting so called.

For an answer, one need look no further than the child-rearing "experts." As the gurus of enlightened parenting, they are the "who." They push the notion that children are ready, eager, and willing to cooperate in their upbringing. Parents need only to reason, use "psychologically correct" communication, and apply the proper techniques. Many, if not most, expert types play down children's inborn inclination to duck and dodge rules and limits.

A college student and young mother asked me, "Do you think children are naturally obedient?"

I answered, "What do you think?" (Therapy 101: Answer a question with a question. I could have instead asked, "What are you being told in your classes?" as I knew the answer to that one.)

She replied, "I don't think they naturally obey. They have to be taught to obey."

"What does your professor say?"

"Just the opposite. And that's the answer she wanted on our exam." How willful.

A child can seem strong-willed by contrast or by context.

Strong-willed by contrast. In any family with two or more children, someone is the tougher or toughest to raise. Spike is actually not all that headstrong, but growing up around Chastity, he looks it, as Chastity is the more easygoing. Compared with her, he appears to be Mr. Hyde, Dr. Jekyll's hard-to-control alter ego.

As parents speak of a child's frustrating contrariness, I ask, "Is there an older sibling?"

"Yes, and Conan is nothing at all like Harmony. He doesn't push us nearly as hard, listens the first time, and takes very little correcting."

"It sounds to me like Harmony is the more typical child. Conan sounds like a mulligan round from God, 'Here, practice on him, I'll send the real kid later.'"

It's shell-shocked second-child syndrome. The first parenting go-around was unusually smooth, making the second seem unusually rocky.

Strong-willed by context. "Do you think your child is strong willed?" Routinely I hear, "Yes, very." Second question: "What does his teacher say?" "She says he's a delight. Gives her no trouble at all. I don't understand that." Last question: "Where did all that strong will go for several hours a day?"

Understandably, most kids are at their most willful with Mom or Dad. Being more secure with us, they push harder on us. Also, they've had years to probe our discipline style, with all its strengths and loopholes. In short, they know us well. Knowledge is power. And power is will.

The law of averages alone would predict that with ten children, we'd have at least one child with a supercharged will, maybe a couple, particularly given their diverse genetics, along with some turbulent histories.

Did we? That depends. (Don't you just love shrinks?) If "strong-willed" is defined as "prone to defy discipline," I wouldn't call any of our children strong-willed. To be sure, some were stronger-willed than others. Some were slower to absorb our teaching. And a few made me consider rewriting whole pages in my books.

Why do I claim no strong-willed kids? Was I numbed by the numbers? Running lower on gas with each addition? Fighting memory slippage?

Perhaps a bit of each, but the primary answer is: The strongest-willed of our children was not stronger-willed than his mother.

The more lovingly confident a parent, the less a child will challenge said parent. Conversely, the less confident, the more he will challenge. Thus, his learning, not his persona, makes him seem strong-willed.

Randi chose to be a stay-at-home mom. To manage a bunch, she knew she had to establish her authority early or chaos would run the day. There was chaos enough without adding unpredictable defiance to the mix. Whatever the discipline—sitting on the steps, standing in the corner, head down at the table, loss of an activity—she made it happen, allowing no fit, fight, or finagle. If so, stronger action followed—no perks or privileges until full cooperation, a swat on the bottom (don't tell the experts), early bedtime. Routine, minor discipline could not be allowed to escalate into a contest of wills. In short, Randi's will to discipline made her need to discipline less frequent.

One morning, breakfast bickering peaked over cereal—who got what and how much. Out came the mini scales and calipers so no one would be slighted half a flake. As two pairs of hands yanked one box in opposite directions, the floor was coated with broken bits of Rice Krispies. Time for Mom to show her will.

Next grocery store outing, as the kids gaped, their mother silently stuffed the cart with several boxes of cereal—all corn flakes; for one month, she did likewise. For weeks, we heard much less snap, crackle, and pop from the kids at breakfast. It was grrreat!

The kids accepted their cereal shortage better than Dad did. Within two weeks, I was groveling, "Randi, I'll give you fifty bucks for one box of Frosted Flakes. Half a box of Golden Grahams?"

When a day's pandemonium reached the decibel level of a 747 Jumbo Jet at takeoff, Mom implemented what she called "Pull the Plug." "Everybody get a book and find a seat"—at the table, on the couch, on the floor. Sit or consequences.

Dump "strong-willed," and you'll be less likely to think little Butch something he's not. Neither will you "pinball-parent"—bouncing from strategy to technique to method, seeking to discipline a child who you think was born to eat discipline for lunch. Then, when someone asks, "Is your child strong-willed?" you can honestly answer, "No more than normal."

Lesson 5

Expect the Unexpected

If you expect the unexpected, is it then still unexpected? Should it happen, it is now expected. Therefore, it is smart to be ready for the unexpected — I mean, the expected.

"You're a psychologist. Aren't you able to figure out kids?" Yes, I am a psychologist, but don't hold that against me. I think I have as much common sense as the next person.

Does being a psychologist give me a third eye to probe deeper into a child's psyche? The book smarts to supply answers to parents whose children are raising question marks? (Doesn't raising any child raise question marks?) Well, yes and no. See, I even talk like a shrink. Leftovers from my schooling.

Being a psychologist might give me some advantage, but it's not an advantage many think of when thinking "psychologist." It is that after I have spent decades talking with and listening to families, my sense of who kids are and what they are capable of has sharpened. Whatever mystifying moves that children — my own too — present don't rattle me quite as much as they might a non-psychologist. Now, that's an unexpected twist, isn't it?

Nearly two hundred child-rearing years (each child equals a minimum of eighteen years) totals one whole lot of surprises — in fact, so many that the younger ones had pretty much lost the

35

ability to shock. They baffled us least. Not because they were better behaved or more predictable, but because Randi and I had
encountered similar stuff from the older ones. A parent can be
jolted only so many times before calming down with, "Oh yeah,
didn't his brother do this too—four times?"

We adopted one of our daughters at age two. Within days of
joining our family, she began to cut her clothes stealthily with scissors. (She was years ahead of current teen fashion chic.) Our initial
solution: Remove all scissors from reach. Problem solved—not
quite. Teeth can function as makeshift shears, though they do
more ripping than shearing. Averse to being the only Cinder-
ella with ragged clothes, she went fang foraging for her siblings'
apparel.

Where was all this coming from? Obviously from her mouth.
Deeper explanations?

a. Adjustment issues

b. Hostility

c. Sibling jealousy

d. None of the above

We knew little of her birth or her two years in foster care. Perhaps a
more detailed history would have afforded some clues. Perhaps not.
Could the split garb be a symbolic expression of a life torn? That
seemed a psychological stretch. My ultimate conclusion: Because.
Aren't you envious of my analytic prowess?

As we didn't rush out for replacements—not until the riddle
was redressed—the originals had to be worn. This made for a
frayed-looking family. One evening after church, an elderly woman
shyly approached us and slipped a ten-dollar bill into my hand,
coaxing, "Buy the children some clothes." When I told my wife
what had happened, she pressed, "Ray, give it back." "I would, but
she's long gone by now. Want to get some ice cream?"

A disconcerting question struck me: What if this sweet lady isn't at the same Mass as us the next week? So I asked Randi, "Would it be tacky to leave envelopes in her pew marked 'Guarendi Garb Fund'?" My wife said nothing, which meant she was saying a lot. I tore up the envelope.

One lunch, our bunch was filling up leisurely at a local buffet—or, as we called it, "throwing out an anchor." With us were friends on their way to having their own bunch. The server gave our group a large table removed from the main eating area. How thoughtful—I think.

Our friend warned us that if we wanted a stress-free meal, her five-year-old daughter would have to sit on her lap every minute, effectively limiting uninterrupted grown-up conversation. "Why is that?" I asked, hoping to gather material for another book. With chagrin and exasperation, she said that "out of nowhere one morning," her daughter became hyper-clingy and demanded, punctuated by meltdowns, that Mom not leave her sight. Overtired? Nightmare? TV viewing? Mom said all that and more was questioned, explored, ruled out. No apparent connection.

She asked me, "What is going on? Is it me? Do other kids go through this?" And most urgently, "How do I stop this?"

Between my trips number one, two, and three to the buffet bar, I asked helpings of questions, seeking some genesis for the abrupt U-turn from carefree little girl to hip hugger. Neither the parents, Randi, nor I could uncover anything, even after two extra visits to the dessert table. That doesn't mean nothing was there. It means we couldn't find it—again, not all that unexpected when living with children and not a creature more predictable, like a timber wolf.

What now? Can a parent solve a baffling puzzle without having all the pieces? If not, lots of kid conduct would have to go unsolved.

Taught by Ten

Mom was nervous that some unseen psychological ferment was buried beneath her daughter's "insecurity," so she hadn't taken firm measures to curtail it. Once she did, her little girl rapidly resumed her old self. (Can you have an old self when you're only five?) The clinging came and went with no clinging aftereffects. One week later, we were all back at the buffet, with the grown-ups at one end of the table and the kids at the other.

Much of the time, a handful of motives accounts for what seems odd or quirky conduct: I felt like it; the idea hit me; I wanted to see what would happen; I thought I could get away with it. In part or whole, these can explain much of the unexplainable.

Juvenile thinking often winds its way through a swirling, whirling, twirling course: Circumstances confront Ripley. A "what if" forms in his head. It does a few back flips and wild lurches and—voila!—out comes conduct that bewilders parents. It may carry little or no masked meaning.

"What you see is what is." This insight no doubt stretches back eons, as a cave father is befuddled as to why his son just scratched off the scene he spent two days drawing on the wall.

My son Andrew, around age four, when asked to explain something puzzling that he did, asked rhetorically from the rear seat of the car, "Who knows the mind of Andrew?" From the front seat, I answered, "Mom does."

One day at preschool, he abruptly grabbed a handful of kernels from the "corn station" and flung them at his station partner. No warning, no provocation, just reflex. His teacher, who reckoned Andrew "socially delightful," was shocked. I wasn't so much. Kids—throwable kernels—impulse—that pretty much summed it up, as I reckoned it. For discipline, his teacher removed him from the corn center to the sand center. Brutal.

Our discipline was a little more hefty, including the afternoon's loss of Mr. *Rogers*—the one showing how TV people put makeup on the Incredible Hulk. I had to watch it all by myself.

On the ride home, I asked Andrew why he chucked the corn, knowing full well that "why" is one of the more futile questions a parent can ask a youngster. As expected, I received a vacant look asking, "Why are you asking me? I'm only the one who did it?" Indeed, a child may not know the why. Or if he does, he's keeping it secret.

Nonetheless, I forged ahead, resolved to penetrate the depths of the corn-kernel caper. After I gave Andrew multiple-choice answers to my why, he obliged with a confession of sorts. "Well, Dad, you tell me some things are good to do, and some things are bad to do. But how can I know which is which until I try them all?" It was shaping up to be one bumpy preschool year.

All of our children gifted us with a healthy quota of "Where's that coming from?" My shrink self said, "Analyze that." My dad self said, "Don't overanalyze that."

"What he did was so out of character. It wasn't him." The bad news: It was him. Who else would it be? At the when and where of the surprising deed, he was the doer. The good news: One or even several "out of character" acts do not a character make. A few pieces of curious, goofy, or odd-looking behavior are not the measure of a child's personality.

What rattles parents is not so much the perplexing behavior itself but the anxiety that it could mean something more, something deeper. What if unseen psychological agitation is percolating? What if it's lurking to manifest itself someday in maladjustment? Ask yourself this question: Is my child pretty "normal looking"? If your answer is yes, then very likely nothing is percolating. The "abnormal" conduct is in the here and now, motivated by who knows what, and it portends nothing for the future. With kids, most often, what you see is all there is to see. The psyche is quiet.

When my children did something inexplicable-looking, I didn't always merely shrug with an, "Oh well, kids will be kids." Though I probably did shrug more than most parents.

Lesson 6

Relax

"He's so different from our oldest and our youngest." "She acts a lot like my sister's daughter, who's also a middle child." "I never put much stock in 'He's the middle child,' but it does seem to fit my son."

Middle Child Syndrome, or MCS—you know a diagnosis has arrived when you can call it by its initials. The profile reads something like this: With neither the privileges given the oldest nor the attention given the youngest, the middle child needs to find his own unique place in the family. Sandwiched between siblings, unsure of his role, he reaches for his fair share of recognition. Misconduct, attention seeking, immaturity—all are ways to proclaim, "I'm here, you know."

The portrait seems plausible. While not fitting every middle child, it appears to fit enough of them to have secured a place in the child-rearing lexicon. There's just one hitch: MCS is not an actual disorder. It's a faux diagnosis.

Experts birthed it, popular media spread it, and parents "saw" it in their middle children. Voila!—an explanation for why Midian is as he is. That is, he's the second of three, or third of five, or fourth of seven. Notice that full MCS can emerge only from an odd number of offspring. If that's your total, here's a sure MCS cure: Have another child. Keep your numbers even.

My theory is that birth-order theories have swelled as families have shrunk. There are now far fewer oldest and youngest children and more older and younger. (Remember your grammar?) Not so long ago, children routinely relocated up and down the family lineup as a new baby arrived, displacing the "old" baby, or as the firstborn flew the nest, moving the second born into the top spot. The larger the family, the more shuffling of place.

As said earlier, Andrew and Hannah were our first two children. Then Sarah arrived, nudging Hannah into the middle, where she sat for two years. Before she could feel any middle-child repercussions, however, Sam came. No longer did we have an actual middle child, but an upper and lower middle.

Fast-forward two years, and Jon and Joanna bumped Hannah two notches higher. Sarah, at age three, dropped two spots, while the twins co-occupied the middle. Sam rested secure as the "baby," but only for about a year. Still with me?

The kids kept swapping positions for several more years. Only Andrew, our first, and Elizabeth, our last, remained fixed in the birth order. All others took turns as the baby, middle child, second youngest, former upper middle.

Over the years, we had four middle children. This raises a question: How long does one have to hold the middle spot to acquire MCS? Can temporarily living in it leave lingering effects?

In fact, birth order is a squishy concept. It doesn't much shape who kids are. It's a popular notion. It sounds plausible, but it doesn't stand up to research scrutiny.

Stereotypes blossom from small seeds of reality. In most three-children families, one child will challenge more than the other two, grab for extra attention, or break more than his fair share of the rules. Chances are 33 percent that he's the middle child. The percentage is high enough to sustain a stereotype. It has little to do with his family position. He'd be that way whether the oldest, youngest, or middle. It's him.

Birth order operates in one place—the oldest or only child—and only slightly. On average, they are a bit more independent, or achieving, or quicker developing. Again, primacy of place may not be the cause. Parents tend to settle into a comfortable rhythm with more children. We did.

With our first, we sterilized everything within fifty feet of him. By our third, we were chiding, "Quit chewing on dirt balls. And go wipe your mouth off with a leaf." Every twenty minutes, we stared wistfully at Andrew sleeping in his crib. A couple of kids later, we were scolding the dog, "Stay out of the playpen, and quit licking him in the face." That latter was a warning to our child. Poor dog.

We had duplicate photos of our oldest's every burp and spit up. Our youngest had one photo at birth, another at graduation. "Hey, Dad, why don't I have any pictures?" "You do, Liz. Your sister did a popsicle stick sketch of you in kindergarten. We kept it. Besides, you look like your sister—use her pictures."

A few months after our ninth was born, someone asked Randi, "Is Petey sleeping through the night yet?" She wryly replied, "I don't know if he is, but we are." Not totally true. I always roused her if I heard Pete fussing.

Parenthood gets more naturally easygoing with more years and more kids. And that's a good thing. Little can chill one's peace more than overthinking and second-guessing every decision or move. Continual self-questioning doesn't raise a parent's competence, only her anxiety.

Suppose God whispered instructions every day into your ears. Wouldn't that guarantee the best outcome? Unfortunately, no. It wouldn't guarantee that young Faith would understand, agree with, or accept your God-given wisdom. Do we grown-ups? Also operating is free will, which even God fully respects. Jesus had a perfect understanding of human nature. Did most people follow Him?

Mistakes—if that is even the right word—are as integral to parenthood as are kids. How could they not be? Especially since another word for "mistake" would be "human."

Let's tally some numbers. Assume only 1 "mistake" per child per day—scolding word, miscalculation, lax discipline. One per day is actually pretty low. With 10 kids, 365 days, 18 years per child (artificial cutoff) the total is 65,700. Given the flow of everyday life—work, school, activities, sleep, bathroom—that number drops as face-to-face time drops. Still, it probably reaches upwards of thousands.

With loving, well-meaning parents, most "mistakes" are minor. They result from contact with someone(s) who needs years of direction but who doesn't always like that direction. And no one—shrinks included—can act decisively when anxious about which moves might trigger a visit to a counselor's couch one day.

"It's as alive for me now as it was then. My mother was in the garage, yelling my name—first, middle, and last—over and over. When I peeked out the door, I saw her shoving my stuffed giraffe deep into the trash can. It was one of my favorites too. I remember bringing it home from the hospital three days after I was born. She was threatening never to buy me another one if I couldn't learn to keep it where people wouldn't trip over it.

I wasn't the same after that. I never hugged another stuffed animal. And in the fourth grade, I counterfeited my first school lunch token."

God must have known who would raise kids—those of us who were once kids ourselves—so He built them not only to survive us but to thrive alongside us. Kids are not made of psychological spun glass. They can be better likened to hard rubber wrapped with steel belts.

The elite child raiser is now thought to be a multiple-degreed, board-certified, child-development specialist with multiple stints on national TV. Mere parents just aren't equipped with cutting-edge child-rearing know-how. Feeling inferior, they too often wonder, "Am I doing this right? Am I missing something? Will I cause the very damage I'm trying to avoid?"

A colleague asked me, "Do you have any regrets as a parent?" "I don't think so." My answer stunned him. He looked as if he were itching to say, "Writing parenting books doesn't make you the perfect parent." I totally agree. In fact, I think I said so in one of my parenting books. What he did say was, "How can you say that? Do you really think you did everything right?" Putting aside just exactly who decides what is "right," my answer reflected my definition of "regret," but obviously not his.

Looking back from this distance, would I do some things differently? For sure. I am infinitely far from infallible, but I acted upon what I knew at the time, using my best judgment. If a decision does not work out, that does not mean it was wrong. To me, regret means acting while caring little about the outcome. It is not acting from human imperfection.

My friend heard me saying, "I've never been wrong." In fact, I was saying, "When I turned out to be wrong, it was not because of intent or apathy." Regrets now can thwart acting well for fear of future regrets.

Epidemic among medical students is a "disease" labeled, not surprisingly, "Medical Students Disease." Its core symptom is the worry that one's aches and pains could warn of something more serious, such as the disorder or disease just studied. In reality, most physical quirks and jerks are transitory and announce nothing worse. Because the doctors-to-be are deluged with all that their body might be saying, however, they overlisten. They become casualties of their own incomplete knowledge. They know just enough to worry too much.

A similar, much more widespread contagion afflicts parents. Call it "Enlightened Parents Disease" (EPD). Its core symptom is a bent to overanalyze what their youngsters' actions might mean, for now and tomorrow. It undermines their peace of mind.

As a psychologist, shouldn't I have a chronic case of EPD? After all, I do have Ph.D. after my name—Prone to Have Doubts?

As a father, the opposite happened. I analyzed less. I accepted better who my children are, and then I moved ahead, not routinely asking, "Is something deeper going on?" With kids, what you see on top is regularly what is down deep.

I didn't do much therapeutic chin stroking, musing, "Well now, that is very interesting." I knew enough not to think too much. Being a psychologist made me a more, not less, relaxed father.

This is not to say, "Most everything kids do tells you nothing." Sometimes it does. (See, my psychologist self is reemerging.) A parenting pitfall, though, is being too quick to read too much, especially into the everyday stuff of kidhood. In a love-filled home, overthinking can mislead more than it leads.

Growing older also brings more easygoingness. It lowers the pressure to be the perfect parent. For our first adoptions, Randi put together "My Storybook," telling of a mommy and daddy who wanted a family and how God gave them one. It was a handsome work with gilt-edged hardcovers and forewords by Mother Teresa and Mr. Rogers. As the kids came faster, though, the picture books got thinner. The last few had two folded pieces of paper, with stick figures drawn by an older sibling. Okay, an exaggeration, but there definitely was some slippage. Fortunately, no younger child seemed to notice. Though a few did complain that the stick figures didn't look that much like them.

Lesson 7

The Affection Connection

"Daddy, I need another kiss goodnight before you go." "Just one more hug, okay Mommy, and then I can sleep really good." "Read me that story again about the superboy and his flying bed."

For little ones, bedtime and bond time blend like a companion blankie and a beloved stuffed companion. "Just one more, Mommy?" however, can become "Two more" can become "Three more," thus awakening a parent to a stall tactic in motion.

Being disciplined can also prompt a call for affection. "I love you, Mommy, and I want to come out of this corner and give you the biggest hug and kiss I ever gave you. Right now, quick, before the feeling goes away ... forever." If that fails, Liberty can always go spiritual. "Can I pray with you too? But I can't do it from way over here." An appeal for affection can be genuine yet hastened by circumstances.

An exception: When temper flares. Meaning to soothe, a parent may meet a warning light flashing, "Don't get too close!" After his temperature cools, though, Blaze is ready to give a green light to being comforted.

On the whole, younger children give and take affection as naturally as they breathe. Seldom do they signal, "Enough already."

Older children, teens by name, don't so readily invite affection, not outside the home anyway. They are known for setting conditions upon a parent's PDA—public display of affection. What's more, teens broadly define PDA. It includes not only touch but also words, gestures, and proper social distance.

"Mom, do you need to keep looking at me so much when we're at the game?" "I'll just walk a few steps behind you, Dad." "It's okay, Mom, to say 'I love you' at home, but you don't have to tell me around my friends." "Please don't hug me every time our team scores."

All like limits are said to protect a teen's primal instinct: to look cool. They are supposedly integral to the adolescent stretch toward grown-upness. Put another way, it's a developmental thing.

My own fatherhood counters this consensus. It's not so much a developmental thing as it is a peer thing. A want—call it a need—for affection is not something kids outgrow. It doesn't weaken with the years. We parents just have to take more initiative, not waiting for an open-armed invite.

My son Peter played high school basketball. Before home games, I would grab a bleacher seat a few rows behind the team bench. Waiting for a pregame opening, I would step down to give Pete a good-luck hug and dad kiss on the cheek. Talk about courting social backlash! No doubt, other parents sat stunned at my brazen breach of the teen code.

Granted, it was a dicey move, but I redeemed it with inspiring cheerleading, "Petey, try not to stink the joint out." Pete heard what I was really saying. "I'm here just to enjoy watching you, no matter how you do." He would retort, "If I do, I'll tell coach how my shrink dad motivates his kids." Pete, in turn, motivated me likewise before my own softball games. It was our mutual hoorah!

After one game, Pete told me that friends had confided to him, "I wish my dad would do that," referring to my open affection. So much for all teens living by the dictate "Don't act like we're related in public."

Many expert types would vote my pregame move a no, as I am to do only what Pete permits. I would vote yes, and it's my vote that counts. I'm Dad.

Pete also ran track. At meets, kids would clump into groups, sending a silent, "Parents, keep your distance." And parents obliged. Not every parent, though. Fully aware that kids prefer to mingle with those their own age and not with us senior citizens, I would nonetheless, every so often, invade their inner circle and wish Pete well with a hug. As his friends watched, accustomed to Pete's pop by now, Pete returned my hug, explaining, "I have to do this, or he'll take my license." Not indefinitely.

The peer rules governing PDA are drifting ever younger. My two oldest children, Andrew and Hannah, attended early elementary school before being homeschooled. Early in second grade, Andrew, getting squeamish over his mother's expressive goodbyes too close to the school's doors, asked to exit the car further back in the drop-off line. Once out of the car, he scampered ahead of his sister, Hannah, who, as a first grader, was not to enter his walking zone.

A few months into homeschooling, however, Andrew's former "assured clear distance" from his mother and sister closed to zero. Apparently he forgot how he was supposed to act. Without classmates looking on, he returned to what once came more comfortably. He and his mother routinely held hands, kissed hello and goodbye, and exchanged "I love yous" – out loud – in public – with people all around. What is labeled "normal development" may be more peer-governed conduct.

Our twins, Jonathan and Joanna, lived through neglect and turbulence, in the womb and thereafter, thus delaying their social maturity and self-control. Consequently, each collected more discipline than their siblings. Some adoption personnel warn: "Wait several months before enforcing rules. Allow the children to settle in." We didn't agree. Without enforced expectations, settling in would take that much longer and be that much harder for all of us. We wanted to enjoy them, not live in indefinite chaos.

After one especially unruly day, however, I asked Randi, "Should we lower our standards for Jon and Jo for a little while, just to lessen their share of discipline?" She replied, "What kind of dumb idea is that?" Okay, she didn't actually say that, but given her eyebrow-raised pause before speaking, she might have been thinking something along those lines.

Rather than lowering our standards, said Randi, let's raise our affection—compliments, hugs, kisses, cuddles. In a flailing attempt to salvage my academic credentials, I countered, "But we already do that." Randi answered, "Then we'll do that more." Who's the shrink in this family? "Let me show you how much I love you" makes "Let me show you how you should act" so much more doable.

In interviews with strong families in my book *Back to the Family*, the parents and children spoke with one voice about affection.

- I can't remember a day that I went to bed without getting hugged and told I was loved.... Our (family) slogan would have been, "If you love someone, *show* them."

- My father is one of the most masculine men I know, but he always kissed my brothers and me, and he would tell us how much he loved us ... even now, a hug from my mother makes me feel good from the inside out, the way it did when I was five years old.

The Affection Connection

- There are times when things are heated, and words just aren't enough. But you can still communicate by touching one another.
- Affection is the quiet language of love.[1]

A word taboo among the gurus of parenting is "punishment." Other, less-harsh-sounding words are to be substitutes — "correction," "guidance," "consequences," "discipline" (though that, too, is somewhat dubious).

The most sophisticated child can't notice the distinction between punishment and correction. "Standing in this boring corner can't really be called punishment. It's more of a correction through a forced change of circumstances. I feel better now."

Parents still punish, despite what it's called. A truly bad punishment, however, is affection withdrawal, however briefly. After facing a major infraction, a parent, not blessed with the divine patience, can be tempted to retreat emotionally, if only to emphasize, "This shows you how upset I am."

If affection comes and goes with a child's good and bad conduct, however, it becomes conditional. If you act right, I'll be warmer. If not, I'll be cooler. Affection is a potent glue in the parent-child connection. It must be absolute.

"I'm not a real affectionate person." "Affection doesn't come easy to me." "That's not my love language." These warrant my sister's one-word comeback when we bickered: "So?"

If something is good to do, it's good to do whether I want to do it or not. It's good to do even if it pushes me outside my "comfort

---

[1] Raymond N. Guarendi with David Eich, *Back to the Family: Proven Advise on Building Stronger, Healthier, Happier Family* (New York: Simon and Schuster, 1991), 149–150.

zone," to use reigning psychobabble. Good parents widen their comfort zones.

If by nature, you're quiet, do you never talk? Are you more talkative with some than with others? If you're a couch athlete, do you never exercise? If you're shy, are you shy with all people in every circumstance or only in some?

"That's not who I am," really means, "That's not who I consistently am." Seldom does it mean, "Never do I do that."

If you're not easily affectionate, do you never touch anyone? A baby? A dog? Do you shake hands? If a guy, do you chest- or fist-bump a teammate? If a woman, do you show a girlfriend small touches of friendship?

Who deserves affection more than your spouse or your children? If only one gesture at a time, affection is a habit that needs to be fed.

Certainly all children don't react alike to affection. And ours were no exception. Still, even those more emotionally restrained would reciprocate at some level if we reached out first.

Want more affection from your child? Discipline better. Use fewer words—nagging, negotiating, warning—and more follow-through. In short: act, don't yak.

"He has told me 'I love you' more in the last two weeks than in the last six months." "She hugged me three times yesterday. I can't remember when that last happened." "He just seems overall more pleasant."

The affection about-face surprises parents. They had expected less warmth with firmer discipline. Instead, they got more. Friction and affection are antagonists.

When spouses are affectionate with each other, the kids feel it too.

When Randi and I hugged, no more than 2.3 seconds later, the littler ones crowded in between us for their share. The older ones, obeying the Adolescent Handbook, page 63, paragraph four-C, "Witnessing Parents' (a.k.a, old people) Affection" felt compelled to comment, "Not again. Aren't you a little old for this sort of thing?"

They had to react so. It was an adolescent reflex. But it was a put-on. They felt secure seeing that the two heads of the family were one.

One father in *Back to the Family* put it this way: "I always knew my parents loved each other. They made no secret of that and, even though we'd say 'gross' when they kissed and hugged each other in front of us, it gave my brothers or me a wonderful sense of security to know they were so firmly anchored in each other."[2]

Generous amounts of affection are all the more meaningful in families raising children with morals high above the culture's. Parents with countercultural standards are routinely misunderstood and critiqued. And the higher those standards, the faster and harder the critiques will come.

When others say, "Live this way" and, refusing to bow to consensus, you say, "I have a better way," your children won't always see the wisdom of your ways either. In effect, they too may accuse, "How can all those other parents be wrong and you be right?" A simple answer: "They are, and I am." Time will prove you right.

And lots of everyday affection will make your high standards that much easier to absorb.

[2] Ibid., 150.

Lesson 8

Authority Is a Good Word

Early psychoanalysts used something called a word-association test. For example, if the analyst said "mother," the patient was to reply with the first word that came into his head. According to Freud, the automatic response would slip through the psyche's defenses, thereby allowing a glimpse into any subconscious conflicts attached to the emotionally charged word.

On or off a psychoanalyst's couch, some words pack more power to conjure up mental connections. For example, if I say "authority," what would you say? "Boss"? "Ruler"? "Control"? Or, would you say, "respect," "love," or "parent"? Most people would reflexively respond with words akin to the first group. Not many would think "respect" or "love."

Authority no longer garners the respect or love it once did. Indeed, among child-rearing analysts, it has gotten quite a spanking. It's judged a throwback word, a leftover from less-informed parenting times. Savvy parents now substitute reason and persuasion. They speak with "I" messages, not "you" messages—e.g., "I'm upset," not "You upset me." They set up win-win scenarios, offering a plethora of choices. They construct deluxe sticker systems. With all these strategies at their command—pardon the authority-sounding word—they shouldn't need to discipline all that much.

And that would be so—if kids saw parenting through our eyes. If they were instinctively reasonable beings. If they were more mature. (Who of us couldn't be?) In sum, if they were more consistently cooperative.

This is not to call the everyday youngster oppositional, or unruly, or strong-willed. (Ugh!) You wouldn't think these words if I said "child," would you? Quite the contrary, it's to call him a child, a normal one who needs a firm hand to grow up well.

Some of the more "nonauthoritative" approaches can work—mostly, though, with Ernests and Angelicas, the "freebies" of child-rearing, those kids who seem to look for ways to make their parents' lives easier. With typical kids, however, they produce mixed success at best. They just don't substitute well for genuine authority.

What is authority not? It is not dictatorship. It is not "Listen up, shut up, and obey." That is pseudo-authority, grounded not in strength but weakness. That is bossiness with little or no warmth.

Authority is expectations backed by fair consequences. It is "Say what you mean and mean what you say." It is a parent's resolve to make and enforce those decisions she judges to be for her child's welfare. Such authority is kind. More than that, it is loving.

"Discipline makes me feel mean"—or to use an "I" message, "I feel mean when I discipline." To be sure, discipline can be mean. It can come with harsh words and inflamed emotions. But that is not so much discipline as it is frustration. Discipline itself is not mean. It is love in action.

Feeling mean, unlike acting mean, undercuts a parent's God-ordained authority. If one feels that discipline is hard-hearted, she will seek to avoid it. In so doing, she will face more undisciplined conduct. And ironically, this will lead to more frustration and, with it, "meaner" discipline.

When Randi and I felt discipline pangs, we reminded ourselves, "If we don't discipline our child now, the world—an employer, a landlord, a sergeant, a police officer, a judge—will one day." And one thing was sure: Our discipline was far gentler than life's would be. Ours came with soft landings.

I was a psychologist years before I was a father. My fatherhood further confirmed for me what I had observed in countless homes—stronger parents have smoother family lives. When young people see that the older people are in charge, they are more settled. Discord drops dramatically, as do the occasions of discipline.

When many experts talk authority, they make sure to soften their language. For example, among those approving of time-out (not all do, as some equate it with isolation and shaming), "brief" is a qualifying word, as in a "brief time-out." Similarly, they cautiously promote this time-out rule of thumb: one minute per year of age.

Among the tiny minority who don't pronounce spanking child-rearing malpractice, the qualifiers come even faster—a "gentle" swat on the bottom, a "light" tap on the hand. The not-so-subtle reminder to parents is: Don't assert "too much" authority.

"One minute per year of age" is a rule we broke. It is too much of a one-size-fits-all misbehavior. Suppose our five-year-old son Jon smacked his little brother in the head—just a hypothetical, you understand. Suppose, too, we made Jon sit for five minutes. What's the unspoken message? "Your brother's hurting head is worth five minutes of your sitting." Our time-out time depended not only on age but on the nature of the infraction and the degree of cooperation. What sort of discipline says, "Sit on the steps, wait for five straight minutes, then you're free to go"?

A timer can help, more so for parents than for kids. Coming home one afternoon, I asked Randi, "Where's Andrew?" "Oh no, I forgot all about Andrew." Heading into the family room, she found him sound asleep in the corner, his head resting securely between both walls. Randi didn't say how long he had been there, but I suspected it was longer than six minutes.

When the day came to discipline my first toddler, I had expected to be ready. After all, I had long touted the benefits of early discipline. That day, though, inaugurated a brand-new fatherhood phase. No more did my little one and I only hug, cuddle, and play. Now I also had to assert my will over his. And it felt a bit foreign. My heart asked, "Is there a way around this?" My head had to answer, "No, this is the right way."

"I wish I didn't have to do this, but I wouldn't be a good father if I didn't." Yeah, like my kids bought that one. Children don't instinctively appreciate a parent's authority, particularly right when it's happening to them. Most will in time, with age, more so as parents themselves.

Parents tell me of receiving from their college student a text (mine to my parents was a letter—how last week!), "Thank you for being the parents you are. Being here, I'm starting to understand why you did what you did when we were growing up." Took you long enough.

Randi and I got a couple of such affirmations. Well, actually, I wrote them and asked the kids just to sign them. One did.

Here's an authority test I give to parents. Next time your youngster does something wrong or bad—can we still use such "value-laden" words?—levy whatever consequence you see fit. "Put your head down on the table, please. When the timer sounds, you can lift it." "Write fifteen reasons why you're grateful to live here." "Hand me your phone, please. I'll decide when it returns."

"Please" doesn't say to a child, "This is a request." It says to a parent, "Stay calm. Let your consequence, not your decibels, do your talking." "Please" doesn't diminish authority. It complements it.

Observe your child's reaction to your discipline. Is it assent, however reluctant? Or is it instant resistance? Argument? Refusal? A demeanor of "No way that's going to happen"? The strength and length of a youngster's pushback measures not so much his willfulness but more his perception of your authority.

What if your test grade is a C or lower, and you'd hoped for an A or at least a B-? Solutions to raising your grade coming up. (Old literary trick: Promise answers shortly to keep the reader reading.)

When discipline is delayed, authority can slip. The longer I waited to act, the more likely I'd fire off something totally unenforceable like "Don't make me come in there, or you two will write an apology longer than *War and Peace*." Really, how could they *make* me come in there?

Sibling quibbling is a common scenario that unfolds so fast that it can stun a parent into discipline inertia.

"Dad, he's making those faces at me again."

"I'm not making any faces at you. I'm just showing you what your face looks like."

"See, Dad, that's how he talks. Then he came over and grabbed my Legos."

"Your Legos? Grandma said they're for both of us."

"I was using them first."

"You were not. They were just sitting there. You weren't even around."

"I was too. I just had to go to the bathroom."

"Oh yeah, for half an hour. Who do you think you are, Dad?"

The discord is stereophonic. Trying to ferret out who did what to whom, why, and how much may be possible with protracted interrogation, but success is more likely at the front end of the clash rather than once it's in full motion.

Ten minutes into one of these "He said, I said, he did, I did," I wasn't likely to warn, "Boys, I'm sensing a lot of irritation. And I myself am feeling anger pangs. Keep at it, and I'm afraid I might raise my voice." Uh huh. Acting early in the chain settles everyone quicker, along with salvaging my credibility.

Much misconduct is not usually one and done. That is, it feeds upon itself, gaining momentum. When Patience nags, she doesn't stop at nag number one. She adds two through infinity until her target—a parent—wears down, gives up, and gives in.

As an aside, doesn't it seem as if kids are slicker than we are? We nag them; they're oblivious. They nag us; we cave.

At the sound of an impending nagfest, Randi's go-to question was: "Are you nagging?" Translation: "Keep nagging, and you'll risk consequences." She knew that the more badgering she endured, the more the kids would badger. It's a simple law.

"Are you arguing?" was another of her question warnings. Mom had neither the time nor the energy to reason with a child who showed no sign of being reasonable, hoping eventually for a meeting of the minds. "Why, thank you, Mother. That's what I was waiting to hear."

To paraphrase a well-known comedian, "I tell ya, authority gets no respect." What was once a well-respected word is being banished to the outskirts of enlightened parenting. And that's not good, for parent or child, because calm, confident authority is a sign of a strong, loving parent.

Lesson 9

The Power of Perception

ME. Did you talk to your mom or dad with the same disrespect
your teen talks to you?
    PARENT. No, I didn't.
    ME. Why not?
    PARENT. I knew.
    ME. You knew what?
    PARENT. I'd be disciplined.
    ME. How?
    PARENT. I don't know.
    ME. Why don't you know?
    PARENT. Because I wasn't disciplined.
    ME. Why not?
    PARENT. Because I wasn't disrespectful.
    ME. Why weren't you?
    PARENT. Because I knew something would happen.
    ME. What?
    PARENT. I don't know.

Our exchange begins to sound like the classic Abbott and
Costello "Who's on first?" baseball comedy routine:
    "Who's on first?"

"That's what I'm asking."

"That's the man's name."

"That's who's name?"

"Right."

Nonetheless, it delivers a big-league pitch—the power of perception.

When I ask a group of parents, "How many of your parents had 'the look'?", heads nod and hands rise. Most know exactly what look I mean. Few recall "My way or the highway" autocrats. Rather, they look back warmly on their parent's unspoken authority.

The look said, "Settle down," "Straighten up," or "Stop now." It signaled, "This is an alert; I'm prepared to act."

The look has relatives: clearing the throat, snapping the fingers, peering over the top of eyeglasses, calling a child by his full name.

"Raymond Nicholas Guarendi!" When my mother in staccato spoke my middle name, I knew I was staring at trouble. For years, I thought that middle names were used only for discipline purposes.

Mothers are said to have eyes in the backs of their heads. I believed this; I still do. My wife could see the kids misbehaving in the van's far-back rear seats even while I was still asking, "Which kids? Where?"

My mother had X-ray vision. She could peer through walls and around corners. I could be hiding under my bed behind a closed door, and she could be downstairs at the kitchen sink. "Raymond, I can see you." How did she do that?

As each child aged enough to present at least a fifty-fifty chance —a coin flip—of making me look good in public, I'd take one along to a speaking event. Extolling on stage the virtues of competent child-rearing, I hoped that child's conduct thirty feet away would validate my words. As I said, a coin flip.

My standard speech runs from thirty to sixty minutes. A standard six-year-old's attention span runs from one to six minutes, unless held hostage by a video game. Keeping my mind focused was tough enough without also straining to catch the eye of a six-year-old boy in the audience making growling race-car noises with his Matchbox car. How did he sneak it past me?

I had to wonder, "How many hearing me are asking themselves, 'Why should I listen to this guy? His own kid doesn't.'"

The look has instant stopping power. A local TV show regularly invited me to talk about parenting. One morning, I decided to walk on the television edge. With bravado, I told Randi, "Don't worry. I think I can take all the kids with me to the show." So I invited not one, nor two, but five children, the oldest being nine, to join me at the studio.

Because the program was live—taped shows do offer some protection through the magic of editing—prior to entering the studio, in my most no-nonsense dad tone, I said what I expected and what they could expect at home should they ignore my expectations. I emphasized also that even while on the set, I could still keep one eye on them.

The interview moved along smoothly enough, and nearing its end, I let out the breath I had been holding since my introduction. The host just couldn't leave well enough alone, as he closed with, "Some of Dr. Ray's children are here with us today. Can we get a camera shot of the kids?" The lens turned toward five children, unblinking and unmoving like Stonehenge monuments. Ten eyes simultaneously fled the camera and stared deer-like at me, as if to ask, "Are we allowed to inhale yet?"

As the camera mercifully returned to me, I sought to salvage the scene. "I think the kids are sensitive to the bright lights." I should have brought along some Matchbox cars, as Randi told me to.

Taught by Ten

Young parents ask, "How did my parents have the look? When I try, I just get a look back like, 'What are you looking at?'" The answer comes from a Russian scientist named Pavlov. Does his name ring a bell?

Pavlov sounded a bell an instant before giving food to dogs. At the first several rings, the dogs salivated only at the sight of food. The bell did nothing. After repeated pairings, though, the bell alone stimulated salivation, as the dogs anticipated food. Psychologists label this "classical conditioning."

The look is a form of classical conditioning. If action follows the look enough times, the look alone succeeds. It's the warning bell.

Rather than being an authoritarian stare down, the look is a gentle warning. It reduces the need for actual discipline. It is a silent cue, substituting for scolding, repeat warnings, or consequences.

Sitting together as a family in church meant finding a long, empty pew. It also meant arriving early, something not easily or-chestrated. Herding young children from point A to point B doesn't progress in a straight line. It's more akin to being trapped in a time warp, in which all motion slows to near zero.

With a child-to-adult ratio of five to one, no seating plan exists that places one grown-up between every two children. And sitting fifteen feet from a small child in a church pew is comparable to sit-ting somewhere in the next zip code on land. Thus, two outcomes follow: his wanting to crawl all over the pew and my wanting to crawl under it.

As more parishioners stared at me, I stared more at the rowdy child. Doing his best to be invisible, he must have still somehow sensed my Clint Eastwood squinty eyes. Either that or a sibling alerted him, "Dad's looking right at you."

Should my gaze fly into space, discipline followed at home, along with, "Did you see me looking at you to settle down in church?" At which, I received a blank look asking, "Was that you?" But after a few more Sunday look–discipline links, the look was all it took.

Parents ask: Why is Gale stormy at home but sunny at school? Why the dramatic temperature fluctuations? A likely explanation: Perception.

A teacher has a mere fraction of a parent's authority. Parents have multiple options for consequences; Mrs. Gradehard has relatively few. Even so, Gale perceives that Mrs. G. has real discipline clout. Beauty is not all that's in the eye of the beholder. So, too, is authority.

Our son Jonathan lived with foster parents for nearly three years. Bedtime there was bad time. Jon refused, resisted, and roamed. The foster parents were sleep deprived.

Our fixed bedtime would upend his preferred day-night cycle. Though we granted wiggle room, no eight o'clock "bedtime ritual" was allowed to stretch toward ten o'clock. That would stretch past my own bedtime.

After a few honeymoon weeks, Jon's former bedtime habits re-awakened. One night, after Randi had tucked in Sarah and Sammy, the youngest ones—and the easiest to put to bed, in my opinion—she turned to me, "Ray, why don't you put the other kids to bed?"

"What?! Does that include Jon? I don't think I have time to-night. I'm working on my parenting book."

Without another word, Randi fixed a "Raymond Nicholas Guarendi" stare upon me. I heard what she was not saying. So I put my manuscript to bed and started collecting children.

"Okay, guys, time for bed." Andrew and Hannah, ages six and five, knew the routine. Jon stood unmoved, as if to say, "Are you talking to me? All I see are your lips moving." So, moving my lips again, "Come on, Johnny, we're heading for bed." Apparently "bed" was a trigger word for Jon, as he promptly dropped to the floor with much weeping, wailing, and gnashing of teeth.

Veterinarians instruct: "Don't corner an agitated animal. Avoid locking eyes with him. Make him see you as no threat." So, using my best no-threat body language, I bent down on my haunches next to Jon and projected a "Let's just all get along" demeanor. Apparently, Jon hadn't read much about animal etiquette, as he howled even louder, hearing none of my soothing words.

So I picked Jon up, effortlessly carting him to his bed. Having lifted weights since college, I know this: I am stronger than even the biggest and baddest four-year-old. Jon would be going to bed. The question was: Under whose power?

Once I had placed him in bed, I held him firmly by his shoulders. My "nonverbal" message: "Daddy means what he says."

Adding words to my muscle, I continued, "Johnny, it's bedtime, son. Daddy is going to hold you here until I think you'll stay in bed by yourself. And if you get out of bed after I leave, I'll come back and hold you longer." His face said, "This is not how bedtime is supposed to go." For Jon's and everyone else's safety, as well as nocturnal peace, there would be no nightly roaming. Behaviorists label my technique one-trial learning. I label it one-night learning.

Andrew was scoping the scene from his perch on the top bunk. "Andrew, would you talk to your brother, please?"

"Jon, if Daddy says stay in bed, you better stay in bed. I remember one time I didn't, and I got in big trouble. Don't think Daddy will go downstairs. He won't. He'll stay up here, out in the hallway to make sure you don't get up. And if you do, he'll be ready for you. Another time I didn't want to go to bed, so ..."

"Okay, Andrew, that's good. Thank you." The boy had a promising future as a lecturing father.

How long did I have to hold Jon until, like a leaking balloon, he deflated? An hour? Half an hour? Actually, it was under a minute.

Had his foster parents done exactly as I did, two minutes could easily become two hours. Because Jon had battled them so hard and long at bedtime, his perception was fixed: "I know the routine. Don't even think you'll keep me in bed." His new family had no such history. And his new daddy made sure our history would start very differently.

Doesn't it seem that life is wired backward? What do little kids resist most routinely? Eating and sleeping. What do grown-ups crave more of? Eating and sleeping. Little kids are one day going to find themselves looking way back with regret, knowing that they once had the freedom to eat and sleep pretty much all they wanted with little or no downsides and that they let it slip by. I know I look back with regret.

When speaking to teachers, only half kidding, I advise: To better manage a disruptive student, begin with perception, specifically his of you. Project complete confidence. Walk it, talk it, breathe it. Spread rumors about yourself the very first week of school. "Mrs. Paddlebottom? I heard she was a mixed-martial-arts champion. In one match, she used a pencil to take down a guy with nunchucks. It's true! I saw some kind of trophy on her desk."

We rescued two Rottweiler puppies. Both are now full grown, and "Tank" weighs nearly what Randi weighs. Yet just the tone of her voice can collar them, as she trained them when they were small. Until she nods "okay," she can halt any ravenous charge toward food. Both dogs are far more powerful than Randi. No matter: they learned early that she is the pack leader.

Once established, perception is durable. A conference once took me away from home for several days. About day three, sixteen-year-old Jon strode into the kitchen close to midnight, surprising his mother. He still didn't like bedtime. "Jon, what are you doing up? Head for bed," Randi directed, while reading his eyes. "Dad's not here. I'm taller and heavier than you, and if I don't want to go to bed yet, what can you really do about it?" She couldn't carry him to bed. For that matter, neither could I anymore. Sensing his male teenage bravado rising, Randi repeated more sternly, "Jon, I said go to bed." After a few seconds of locked looks, Jon slowly retreated and trudged begrudgingly up the stairs.

Had his mother not solidified her authority back when he was a pup, her command would have been empty. Jon didn't want to back down, but echoing in his mind was, "What will happen if I challenge her?" That, and he also knew she'd tell Dad.

When I speak as a psychologist, parents don't need to heed me. When I speak as a father, my children do need to heed me. Otherwise, my book learning will carry me only so far, and that may not be far enough. The more a parent has perceived authority, the less she has to use that authority. Her look may often be enough. So to quote Humphrey Bogart in *Casablanca*, "Here's looking at you, kid."

Lesson 10

K.I.S.S.

Have tokens, will travel—a calling card from my psychology youth. It speaks of a system that rewards good (oops, "appropriate") behaviors with tokens and withholds them for bad (oops, "unacceptable") behaviors. Known as behavior modification, it parallels real economies, hence the name: token economy.

While tokens are its standard currency, others can substitute—points, money, stickers, thumbs up. Sticker charts are a favorite of parents with young children.

A scenario. Mother wants five-year-old Dawn to make her bed without prodding each morning—or, at a minimum, to make an age-worthy attempt. She is weary of opening the day with requesting, reminding, and rerouting Dawn back to her bedroom. A friend suggests, "Have you tried rewards?" So, diving into the Internet, mom searches "Bed-making strategies for children." Finding a lengthy list of "proven reward techniques," she narrows her quest to "sticker reward charts," selecting one with five-star parent ratings. (Are stars grown-up stickers?)

Following its step-by-step directions, with fanfare mom uses colorful magnets to stick her finished chart to the refrigerator. My estimate is that 92 percent of all such charts occupy the fridge's door. That probably has something to do with its being the most sought door in the house.

Dawn's calendar sits ready for her daily rewards, stickers chosen from an ample array of ballerinas, bunnies, superheroes, and scratch 'n' sniff options. Mom sets a goal of five stickers, which Dawn can cash in for assorted perks and privileges. Should Dawn leave her bed bedraggled or slip into her former finagling, her day will be stickerless. The idea is that Dawn will work for stickers more than she won't work for a neat bed.

If the chart does its job, Dawn will do hers. The satisfaction of a job well done will eventually replace any need for stickers.

That's the theory anyway—on paper or, as it were, on the refrigerator door.

Have I designed similar systems? In my early years as a school consultant, yes. In my early years as a parent, no. Why not? For several reasons.

One, the assumption behind such systems is questionable. One theory says that once the habit is formed, the rewards motivating it can be tapered. A counter theory says: Taper the rewards, and the habit itself will taper. Not always do external rewards lead to internal motivation.

Two, any system requiring ongoing monitoring can also invite fatigue. Over time, supervision slips. "Mom, you didn't give me my sticker for today or yesterday." "I know, Justice, I forgot. And I need to buy some more. What if I just draw you a smiley face instead?"

Based on my eyeball analysis of fridge doors, the average lifespan of a sticker chart is twenty-five to thirty days, or just about the time a second calendar is due to go up.

Three, novelty excites—at first. Collecting stickers or any new reward is exhilarating—for a while. What once thrilled loses luster, however. The rush loses potency and, with it, motivating power.

K.I.S.S.

Within the first few months of first grade, our daughter Hannah had earned forty-nine erasers, each one grabbed from the "goodie bag" for every book read. As her stockpile of erasers rose, Hannah's hankering for them fell.

Her mother and I decided to thin the pile. For one reason, reading is its own reward. Hannah didn't need an extra push for something that came naturally. For another, forty-nine is about forty-seven too many. Hannah was to pick two favorites and return the rest. This no doubt puzzled her teacher, who probably thought we were quasi book burners. Not really, just eraser returners.

Ironically, these systems may reward a parent more than the child. That is, they structure some consistency: If Dawn does X, parent does Y. Conversely, if Dawn doesn't do X, parent doesn't do Y. The system mandates it. If it nudges a parent to act more and talk less, it helps—again, for a while, until boredom or fatigue sets in.

Early in fatherhood, I learned this about myself: The easier it is, the more likely I am to do it. The more likely I am to do it, the better it works. The better it works, the less I have to do it.

Our make-your-bed rule was simple: Bed first, fun after. Make a genuine, age-decent effort, even if at first only pulling up the covers, which paralleled my own skill level. When a bed was left looking as if it had been slept in, the rule kicked in. Within minutes, a child who "forgot" remembered. It was a miracle.

"I can't always keep track of my discipline—what, when, and for how long." "When is Faith's grounding over? She says tomorrow, but I thought it was next week." "Does Newton get TV as soon as he's done with his math or with all his schoolwork? I don't remember exactly what I said. He says it's just the math." "How long was Edgar Allen's written apology supposed to be? Why again does he have one?"

To limit our memory lapses, whenever possible, we sealed our discipline with a K.I.S.S.: Keep it simple and sure. Simple promotes consistency and predictability. For most daily trouble spots, we relied upon a handful of easy, go-to consequences: standing in the corner (time begins when quiet), head down at the table (with or without timer), writing sentences or "better behavior" essays (conscience on paper), extra chores (labor).

Corner time for younger kids is about as basic as it gets. Most rooms have at least four corners, all within easy eyesight. Fill them, and another room is only feet away. Should our corners get backlogged, I sent out notices: "Show up tomorrow at 4:00 p.m. You have corner time."

Corners are the ideal time-out spots, as they are quite boring. Other time-out options — chairs, couches, steps — allow for some distraction and amusement. Our kids asked for the steps over the corner, as they could while away the minutes watching life around them. Even watching their siblings was more interesting than staring at the intersection of two walls.

Corner time is repeatable and particularly useful for high-frequency misbehaviors — sibling quibbling, temper tempests, homework hassles, chore shirking, meal melees, toy litter. Corners confirm a discipline truth: A simple consequence used consistently works better than a fancy one used inconsistently.

God runs the world with ten basic rules. A house is a far smaller place. Though, according to the comedian Stephen Wright, "It's a small world, but I wouldn't want to paint it."

For Randi and me, house rules were an oil that made our days run more smoothly. A sampler: You hit, you sit. You fight, you write. You're mean, you clean. You shirk, you work.

Occasionally, we turned to a major consequence: blackout. Blackout was complete cessation of all perks, privileges, and activities—except love, some kinds of food, and okay, the bathroom. For those younger, this included but was not limited to toys, games, videos, television, stuffed animals, dessert, favorite cup, favorite shirt, outside. Books were not banned.

For those older, blackout included any of the relevant above, along with transportation, technology, money supply, outside activities.

Because blackout was our most potent discipline, it was a response to heavier misconduct. Lying, for example, led to an automatic one-day or longer blackout, depending on the extent of the deception. So, too, did physically assaulting a sibling. With blackout as a potential consequence for more serious stuff, more serious stuff happened far less often.

Blackout could be time limited or open-ended. One of our daughters, around age thirteen, dug herself into a money pit with some overdue library books. I would have noticed, but I was preoccupied with writing my article "Teaching Teens Fiscal Maturity."

Spying thirty dollars on our dresser, she spied a quick fix to her fix: Collect my money to cancel her fines. She placed the money in an envelope and wrote a note that said something like, "Dear librarian, I'm sorry that I kept these books for so long. Here is money to pay for all of my fines, and if it's more than you need, please use the extra to buy books for the library."

How did we find the envelope? My wife saw it sitting on our daughter's dresser when delivering laundry to her room. This raised the question: Did she want to get caught?

The incident was not without its positives. Our daughter did express remorse. Her letter was grammatically correct, one result of her discipline essays being Mom corrected. And she did show a generous spirit, although moved by my money!

After a heart to heart, we implemented blackout. Its conditions: contrition (not always easy for a parent to know), cooperation, and pleasantness. Any "This is so unfair" attitude would only prolong her time.

Blackout would have been lifted after about a week, but she covertly transgressed again. Though we didn't detect it, another person did—her younger sister. Kids routinely know what their siblings are up to, more so than do their parents.

Now a young woman, this daughter not so long ago asked me, "Dad, was my blackout the longest in our family?" "I'm afraid so. Since everybody is grown, there's no chance it will ever be topped." I did sense a bit of pride hiding in her question.

"My child really resists being disciplined." Exasperated parents tell how their child negotiates, argues, ignores, erupts, or straight-out defies. Buck refuses to stand or stay in the corner. Page turns her written apology into a written diatribe. Telly won't surrender her smartphone after seriously misusing it.

One potent response to a direct challenge to a parent's authority: immediate blackout, in place until Harmony accepts her initial discipline. Once she is pleasantly cooperative, her blackout is lifted.

Did we ever reward with stickers, treats, money? Yes, but with a variable-ratio-reinforcement schedule, as behavior psychologists label it. Stripped of its heady-sounding language, it simply means "rewards at random."

All slot machines work on a variable-ratio schedule. Because a player can't know when he might win, to win sometimes, he has to play many times. Thus, he will yank levers and push buttons until tendinitis sets in. Pigeons pecking for seeds dispensed on a variable-ratio schedule will drop from exhaustion.

We took a lesson from Vegas. At random, we would "pay off." "Hey everybody, we're heading out later for ice cream. You've been doing great with your [chores, schoolwork, getting along, picking up, burping more quietly at the table]."

My nagging fear is that one of these days, our grown children will be looking at a slot machine and realize, "Hey, they used this stuff on us. We were their pigeons." Not always.

Lesson 11

The Power of Perseverance

The attorney's suite was tastefully pristine. The end tables were without scratches or rings left from sweating glasses abandoned on them by juvenile hands. Each lampshade rested ramrod straight over its matching chic base. No milk, jelly, or pet residue mottled the carpet. Like an out-of-country tourist, I gaped at this picture straight off the cover of *Better Offices Today*. My wife noted, "Some houses look like this inside." I nodded, "I've read about them."

The receptionist welcomed Randi and me with a smile. It lingered as the first two little children trooped in on our heels. With children number three and four, her expression did an about-face, as if asking, "Is this some kind of club?" When the kid coterie hit seven, her eyes left us to scan the room, doing a quick calculation, "How much can they depreciate our office in the hour they're here?"

I intruded on her fretful musing with an "Okay, everybody, find seats." Like a football team breaking from a huddle, all scrambled for positions. At which, the receptionist remarked, "I'm impressed."

"Thanks," I said. "But you've only seen today. You haven't seen all the previous days when I've said the very same thing and got looks of 'You mean me?'"

Why did "Find seats" find cooperation? It was the end result of perseverance. That is, should a child be slow to find a seat when asked, he'd find himself sitting longer later at home. After enough follow-throughs, the stiffest seat resister preferred public seating over home seating.

Had I abandoned my "Sit now or sit later," on the fifth or the twenty-fifth try, I would have sent the message: You resist, I'll desist. After which, no receptionist would be impressed. And who knows how much depreciation I'd have to pay for.

Even with the rolling tsunami of "right now" e-mails, texts, and social media, some people still choose to talk with others on a phone. How last week! "Quiet, please, I'm on the phone" are fighting words for kids, cueing them to interrupt with assorted gestures, handwritten requests, or Marcel Marceau–like pantomimed pleas. Static-charged conversations are enjoyable for neither the caller nor the callee.

They call for dialing up "the look." Whoever is listening on the other end, no matter how tightly your hand covers the mouthpiece, can likely still hear your heated words aimed at the kids. But she can't hear your look. To make your look do your talking, try this:

"Alexander, Belle, when I am on the phone, you are to be quiet. Do not interrupt me unless it's an emergency. And 'I need to ask you something right now' is not an emergency. If you get loud or rude, I will excuse myself from the call and send you both to your rooms. I will come to get you whenever I'm done. Come out before that, and you'll be grounded for the day."

Parents ask, "How many times will I have to do something like this before I get cooperation?" Striving to be precise, I reply, "If you're lucky, once. More likely ten times. Possibly even twenty—I really don't know. That'll be eighty dollars." The number isn't what's important. The will to persevere to phone peace is. Then your look alone will bring the sounds of silence.

Give up after two or three calls, though, and your agitation may be heard loud and clear. "Oh hello, Deacon Gideon, how are you? ... Absolutely, we would be flattered to be the role-model family for the church-children gala. ... I agree, children are gifts. We often wish we had twelve or thirteen more. ... Deacon, can you excuse me for just one second, please? I need to have a brief love chat with the children. They're getting antsy. We're a half hour past prayer circle, and today's the day we pray in Aramaic. Hold on, I'll be right back. Thank you. Peace to you, Deacon — Harmony, Aquarius."

With the phone at arm's length and your jaw clenched, an off-call monologue begins: "Leave her alone, you little weasel. Now! You better hope I never get off this phone. Make me look bad to Deacon Gideon, and I'll ground you until you're married. If we lose the Faithful Family Award because of you two ..."

Returning to the phone, "What's that, Deacon? Oh, that's our neighbor lady. It's sad, but she does talk to her kids that way. ... Well, I do try to set a good example for her. ... And we do pray for her. ... Certainly, I'll invite her to the gala, but I don't think she'll come. Kids seem to bother her."

The power of perseverance rests upon this question: Perseverance in what? Perseverance in words — nagging, cajoling, pleading, over-reasoning, yelling, re-re-reminding — only leads to more words, not results. Perseverance of this sort is worse than futile. It is counterproductive. It teaches Alexander and Belle to ignore or defy.

A father told me, "I follow your advice. I just keep telling my kids over and over as long as it takes." I'm not sure exactly what advice he heard from me, but I thought: As long as it takes for what? Exasperation? Exhaustion? Eruption?

Words may sound like discipline, feel like discipline, even get some compliance if said with enough volume. Words, though, are a counterfeit of discipline. They talk a parent into thinking she's persevering.

Should I be able to give a parent multiple discipline options, I can't give him the will to act on them. If he has the will to discipline, and the kids know that, he will discipline less. Good parenthood is not only knowing what to do; it is also doing what you know.

"I've tried everything; nothing works. Finally, I got so frustrated that I sent him next door to play and moved the family while he was gone." Actually, I haven't heard about any parents stealthily relocating while a child was at the neighbor's. I would guess a few have fantasized about it.

As Mom or Dad lament how they've timed out, turned off, talked loud, and taken away every privilege except breathing, along the way they tried much that would have worked. They weren't consistent enough for long enough. They prematurely assumed that had they found just the "right" approach—the "psychologically correct" discipline—Candy would be much sweeter by now and Sandy would clean his room before mold sets in. Consistency in follow through is fundamental. But consistency is perfected by its partner—perseverance.

We live in a microwave culture. We want results now, with minimal effort. How long is this going to take?

To heat my coffee in the microwave, I tap in sixty seconds. Around the thirty-second mark, I'm pacing back and forth like a caged panther and accosting the timer, "Come on. Pick it up. I haven't got all minute."

Are you Catholic? Do you frequent Confession? Have you done so for years? Do you begin, "Bless me, Father, for I have ... well, maybe you can just bless me because I really can't think of that many sins to tell you anymore. You see, I've had decades to conquer them, and if I haven't by now, well, something must be wrong with me."

Or are you like I am? "Bless me, Father, for I have sinned, and I have my written list with me to refer to. It pretty much covers what I've been confessing forever."

When I act wrongly, I invite discipline. Someone criticizes me, my conscience harasses me, life itself teaches me. For decades, I've been receiving the results of my misbehavior. When will I learn? How long is this going to take?

Parenting books tout the rapid results of their counsel. "Ten Right-Now Ways to Get Kids to Listen." Speed is a major selling point. And when read about in a book, the strategies sound fast-acting. My children have taught me to read reality. Whatever methods I use, I must persevere with them, not for weeks or months but, if necessary, for years.

No matter how long ago troublesome conduct has disappeared, it can reappear. A respectful child can get disrespectful when emotions run high. Siblings can get along well until they don't. Venus thinks Mom a goddess until she denies her a "must-have" freedom.

Persevering when persevering no longer seems needed is absolutely vital to raising a morally mature, virtuous young person.

As that great ball player and life philosopher Yogi Berra once observed, "It ain't over till it's over."

Lesson 12

Talk Less to Be Heard More

Coming home one afternoon, I counted five kids scattered in sundry pursuits. Six-year-old Andrew was missing from the melee.

"Where's Android?" (A nickname.)

Randi replied, "I sent him to his bed."[3]

"What did he do?"

"He lied to me."

Marriage tip for husbands: Upon entering your house and seeing your wife exhausted from having refereed assorted feuds and fracases, do not project an air of "I'm home. The children will now receive proper parenting." It is smart to give a spouse support. It is dumb to act superior.

"Would you like me to talk to him?" (Note the sensitive counselor speak: How might I help?)

Randi nodded toward his bedroom. I read that as "Do your dad thing."

---

[3] We didn't buy into the nonsense notion that sending a child to his bed or bedroom for time-out would foster bad feelings toward a good place. I visited my bed against my will many times as a kid. I love my bed.

Andrew was lying on his bed, intently studying the ceiling, no doubt in musing remorse over his recent transgression. Skipping chitchat, I moved right to my mission.

"Andrew, Mom tells me you lied."

"I don't remember."

Had he been secretly watching cross examinations on Court TV?

"Andrew, if Mom says you lied, you lied. If you lie to me, now you have two lies and more trouble. So think again, did you lie?"

"I still don't remember, but if Mom says I did, there's probably a pretty good chance I did."

He was pleading the Fifth while semi-confessing—a clever dodge. I felt a cognitive tingle. The time had come for my first prolonged foray into fatherhood oratory.

"Andrew, look at me, son." Once assured of his full attention, I launched. I spoke of the value of integrity, of one's word being his bond. I recounted lying to my father at his age and how much I had disappointed him. My finale was an emotional appeal to trustworthiness. At one point, I thought about pulling several nose hairs to make my eyes water. I didn't. Andrew would have seen through that. Besides, it hurts.

Our hearts had touched. Our souls had merged. Ten solid minutes of paternal love coupled with monologue moxie. Andrew couldn't help but be hypnotized.

Years into the future, God willing, as our family collected around the Thanksgiving table, Andrew would share, "I've never told this to anyone. I was only six years old when Dad and I had a talk that altered the course of my young life . . ."

After my mass of words, I gave Andrew the last word. "Andrew, is there anything you'd like to say?"

"Uh huh. Dad, how come if my one eye looks at the ceiling, my other eye can't look at the floor?"

Somewhere in my mini speech, I lost that boy, and I suspect it was right after saying, "Andrew, look at me, son."

My book *Back to the Family* presents the findings of a three-year nationwide search for strong families. More than one hundred families—parents and children—were interviewed and asked, "What makes family life good?" When we asked the kids, "What do your parents do that you dislike?" we heard, "They lecture."

Kids define "lecture" narrowly. To them, a lecture is anything over fifty words, two or more compound sentences, or beyond one minute long. It opens with, "We'd better talk"; "You need to listen up"; "What were you thinking?"; "I'm not talking just to hear myself talk"; "When I was your age ..."

Parents define "lecture" much more broadly: minimum one thousand words, ten minutes or more, and five or more grunts from its hearer to signal he's still conscious.

A lecture staple is the childhood contrast. Its objective is to convince Eden just how good she has it.

"You think you've got it tough? Let me tell you what tough is. When I was your age, I used to walk six miles to school through a foot of nuclear waste. We had one pair of shoes for seven kids, and my turn came around only every Tuesday. And I always gave my turn away. That's the kind of child I was."

"I got up at five o' clock in the morning—two hours before I went to bed the night before—for breakfast split a corn flake with three brothers, carried them to school on my back, and did their homework along the way. And you know what else? I was grateful for what little I had."

"What did you have, Dad?"

"Nothing! Weren't you listening?"

Childhood contrasts have probably been around for thousands of generations. Somewhere long ago, a caveman could be heard grumbling, "These kids, nowadays. All they want to do is sit and stare at the fire. I tell them, 'You go find food first and then you can watch the fire.' Now they all want to wear something they call shoes. I tell them, 'These things are nothing but a fad.' But do they listen?"

Has the childhood contrast seen its day? What will our kids tell their kids? "Five hundred fifty channels—that's all we watched when I was a child. The TV screen covered barely half the wall, in only two dimensions. All six of our remotes had power buttons up at the top. We had to stretch our thumbs to turn them on. Sometimes my joints got sore."

"One winter, it snowed so bad that my mother shoveled only half the walk before she collapsed. I had to walk around her with my hot chocolate—almost spilled some on my hand." Just doesn't have the same oomph, does it?

My kids believed all I had to worry about was dodging dinosaurs and not burning my feet on the still-cooling earth.

Lectures are driven by the desire to be understood. We so much want to convince Earhard that we're not bucking for "Tyrant Parent of the Decade." Rather, we are talking toward his own good. If we could find just the right words, the flawless logic, and mix in a few "I" messages and win-win scenarios, a light would flicker in Iris's eyes, and we'd be honored with, "I can see clearly now, Mom. You make so much sense. Twenty minutes ago, I wasn't with you. Thank you for twenty minutes more until I finally realized what you're saying."

Not all lectures fall on blocked ears. Along the child-rearing way, it's wise to explain ourselves, sometimes in detail, even if unheard. Most lectures, however, obey the law of diminishing returns. They reach a point where our voice is heard only by us.

Most of my monologues covered the same turf—sibling quibbling, homework hassles, chore shirking, ruined rooms, anemic gratitude, poor manners. The kids already knew much of what I was about to say. They could write most of my script. Or feed my teleprompter.

I would often ask myself, "Why does it take so long for me to get through?" Then just as often I wondered, "Is God asking the same about me?"

It's not that the kids didn't understand me. They didn't always agree with me. If they had, my parenting would have gone a whole lot smoother. On the first morning of first grade, as each child walked out the door, I could counsel, "Remember now, always do your schoolwork. You don't know what you'll want to do twelve years from now. So keep all your options open."

"Thank you, Father, for the good guidance. You can count on me." And enough said.

During counseling, a mother is convinced that no matter how well she explains herself, her daughter Joy just can't fathom why she is "stricter" than her friends' parents, is slower to give techno perks, and swims against the cultural flow. Turning to Joy, I ask, "Why does your mom do what she does?" Whereupon Joy explains, reiterating in detail what Mom has told her repeatedly. After being revived with smelling salts, Mom manages to mumble, "I can't believe she thinks that." I add, "She doesn't, but she knows that you do." Lectures aim to foster understanding. They're less fruitful at fostering agreement.

Did I overtalk until the day—and beyond—my last child left home? Yep. Lecturing is a dominant gene in a parent's DNA. However frustrating and futile, it is well-intended. That said, and said again, my frequency and length dropped with the years and number of kids.

On occasion, the younger kids overheard me talking at the older kids. So, agree or not, they vicariously absorbed some of my words. Call it lecture by osmosis.

Then, too, I learned to read better the signals of a drifting audience: subtle nonverbals, such as eyes glazed, crossed, or closed; and verbal ones, such as "I know, Dad," "You've told me this before," or "Where's Mom?"

A final word, lest I've already gone on too long. To paraphrase an axiom: One consequence is worth a thousand words. More teachable than talk is action. If it's worth talking about, it's worth doing something about. Lectures aim to make the point. Discipline brings the point home.

Lesson 13

Respect the Power of Respect

Pulling up the driveway as my wife was stepping into the garage, I had a vague sense that something was amiss. Fortunately, years of sharply honed powers of observation have enabled me to read the most subtle of spousal signals.

In Dr. Seussian rhyme, Randi was repeating, "I do not like it, Ray I am. I do not like her attitude. I do not like her sour mood. I do not like it here or there. I do not like it anywhere."

'Long about her third verse, I was definitely convinced something wasn't quite right, so waiting for a lyrical pause, I interjected, "Are you upset?"

"It's Sarah." (Our then thirteen-year-old.)

Just then Sarah joined us. "What should I do now, Mom?"

"Well, Sarah, you can sweep out the garage and then vacuum the living room."

"What's this about?" I asked.

"I gave Sarah two hours of labor." Labor in our home meant chores assigned because of misconduct. The benefit was twofold: teaching a child and trimming our workload. While laboring, stumbling and mumbling zombie-like was unacceptable. A victimized, put-upon pout only risked added chores. "Whistle while you work" was the goal but was seldom reached.

The kids once conspired to unionize but fell short one vote. We could still buy off the young ones with promises of ice cream and gummy bears.

Two hours of labor was a hefty chunk of time, so I asked Randi, "What did Sarah do?"—expecting to hear something like, "She spray-painted in capital letters on the driveway 'Mom is clueless.'"

Instead, Randi said, "She rolled her eyes at me."

Two hours for rolled eyes? That's one hour per eye. Is this because eye rolling is so disrespectful? Yes, but even more so, it's because Sarah's mother deserves Sarah's respect.

So says God. Indeed, He devotes a full 10 percent of His commandments to honoring one's father and mother.

Whatever its mode—words, tone, looks—unchecked disrespect feeds upon itself. It can mutate into a style so habitual that it numbs a parent. It ceases to register.

A scenario: Dawn slouches into the kitchen late on a school morning. Her mood is sleepy and surly.

MOM. What time did you get to bed last night?

DAWN. I don't know. Sometime. (*Undertone: Don't talk to me.*)

MOM. I was just wondering because you really look sleepy.

DAWN. I'm not, okay? And don't start with my phone and bedtime.

MOM. I didn't say a word about your phone. I know you have a test today; I just hope you're ready.

DAWN. My grades are fine, and I don't need you to keep nagging me about them.

MOM. You watch your mouth, Dawn. I'm just trying to help.

DAWN. Yeah, like your lectures help. I need some toast; I have to go.

MOM. What kind did you want? It'll take a few minutes.

DAWN. Forget it. I don't have time.

MOM. I can get you a muffin.

DAWN (*heading for the door, back to mom*). Never mind.

Mom is singing, "Give Peace a Chance" as Dawn is singing, "Hey You, Get Off My Cloud." By my count, Dawn is snotty at least four times. Mom gamely struggles to return nice for nasty. Dawn responds with a generic, "You're annoying."

After the third go-around, Mom warns Dawn. Dawn snarks through it, confident she'll face no repercussions. Back home in the p.m., she could resume where she left off in the a.m. should Mom once again engage her. I mean, how much can Dawn be expected to endure?

It's the "Battered Parent Syndrome." Mom has been accosted so rudely and so often that, like developing tolerance to a drug, she no longer feels any effect.

A second scenario: A parent and teen are in my office. As parent speaks, teen "corrects" with a collection of "Yeah, right," "Whatever," "That's wrong." After several such interruptions, I ask, "Do you hear how your son is talking to you?" Sometimes, the parent is embarrassed at my hearing what he doesn't. And sometimes, he is angry: "You're right. I think I've been allowing it because I've just gotten so used to it."

"Let children express themselves": so express counselors. Good practice, up to a point. Not all expression is civil expression, however. The right to free speech comes with conditions. And you are the one who sets those conditions, not some expert who—may I assume?—doesn't live in your home or share your values. You draw the line separating "Here's what I think" from "Here's what I think about you."

"Sometimes, Dad, I just don't get why you do what you do. I can't see why I don't have a smartphone when every one of my friends does. I know you tell me, but I still don't understand."

"I can't believe you. You make rules just to show who's boss. Every one of my friends thinks you're totally ridiculous for not giving me a smartphone."

Both sentiments are openly expressed, only one diplomatically so. Which one is diplomatic is obvious. It's not always obvious, though. The boundary between "I feel" and "Get real" can be fuzzy. To set a clear boundary, do an experiment.

For one month, imitate Oral's expressive style with your best friend, boss, or pastor. Should they say or do anything you find disagreeable, sigh heavily, roll your eyes, and add a "Whatever." At the end of the month, ask each, "Do you still like me?"

What experts often call "free expression" from child to adult, if practiced adult to adult, would damage, if not destroy, a relationship.

Let children speak their minds—my college professors' mantra. Speak your mind so long as it's spoken with respect—my parents' mantra.

Whose mantra did I follow—my profs' or my parents'? I went with how I was raised.

Little children lean toward theatrics to express their displeasure, emitting sounds not heard in nature, torquing limbs like the old kids' toy Gumby, and leaking fluid from facial orifices. Were I to fling myself on the floor with the freewheeling abandon of a three-year-old, I'd be stranded down there until someone rescued me.

"Ignore young children's temper outbursts. They're normal. They'll be outgrown," parents are told. They may be normal, but normal doesn't mean good.

Let-it-all-hang-out eruptions, if allowed to run freely, aren't usually outgrown. They may be still rocking the house when Tempest
is six, eleven, seventeen. "Ignore it" was advice we ignored.

For years, we had at least four children under age five. If each
child emotionally melted down only once per day—a low number—and each meltdown lasted several minutes, the total temper
time would top a half hour per day. That's way too much heat for
us—and them too.

Watching, the older ones would have been quick to accuse,
"You never let us act like that." Doesn't it seem that kids keep a
secret diary of every time and place they were disciplined for the
same thing their younger siblings aren't?

As kids get older, they rely more on words than on melodrama
to express discontent—more speech than screech. They are skilled
at tap dancing right up to the line dividing nice from nasty, every
so often stretching a toe past it to check if it has moved any.

I ask parents, "Is backtalk a problem in your home?" We don't
permit it.

"What do you do if it happens?" We make it clear it's not
acceptable.

"What do you do about it?" We warn him, "Watch yourself,
young man."

"What do you *do*?" We let him know in no uncertain words
we won't tolerate that kind of attitude.

After my third or fourth, "What do you *do*?", a parent hears
what I'm asking, and it's not "What do you say?"

Repeated warnings are not discipline. They may sound like
discipline, but that's all: They *sound* like discipline. Kids are quick
to gauge how much talk will proceed any action.

The myth says: Limit Gabby's free speech, and she will become a stifled, robotic child. Forced into self-restraint, she will

stew silently and resentfully. Her thinking will be, "I'll obey you. For now."

In fact, the opposite is true. Mutual respect leads to less friction and less hurt for all parties. The most permissive parent eventually reaches her limit. Few people—and parents are people too—can absorb ongoing mistreatment from anybody, young or old.

"I don't like how I talk to my children. I don't talk to anyone else the way I talk to them. Sometimes I can be downright mean."

A more respectful child raises a more respectful parent. When not receiving lip, one is far less likely to give lip. Speaking politely comes more easily when one is spoken to politely.

In our family, respect was not only vertical—child to parent and parent to child—but also horizontal—child to child. All family members were to treat everyone well—or, at a minimum, not poorly. It was an absolute, one that was absolutely enforced.

Of course, the sounds of sibling strains are regularly muted, silent even, making oversight less than perfect. Three-year-olds believe that grown-ups are all-knowing. By age four or five, they realize, "Hey, I just did something wrong, and no one caught me. This changes things."

So far as we could enforce, sibling agitating was forbidden. Taunts, name-calling, put-downs, assaults, jumping off the ropes into the ring—all met rapid response from Mom or Dad, whoever sensed it first, which usually meant Mom. The kids may have outgrown the belief that "Mom sees all." I never did.

Children are masters at bending the rules without breaking them. Once Jon came to us complaining, "Andrew is calling me a name." Confronted, Andrew confessed. He had, in fact, been repeating, "Jon's a name." Which raised the question: Can you discipline for no actual wrongdoing but only intent?

To limit sibling squabbling, we once more stuck with the simple: separation to neutral corners, loss of perks or privileges, handwritten letters of apology, assuming the aggrieved party's chores, writing fifteen positives about a sibling. Positives couldn't be reverse negatives, as in, "He doesn't smell like a goat all the time." Or, "She's really good at getting away with stuff." Which then prompted one sibling to ask, "Can I make up stuff then?"

"Let children solve their own disputes. It teaches them conflict resolution skills," the experts intone. Do these folks have more than one child?

Child-directed "conflict resolution" can work, given certain conditions: All pugilists are equal in age, in size, in feistiness, in smarts. If not, the "more equal" child will win. He will resolve the conflict in his favor.

With ten children, all possible combinations of who did what to whom, when, where, and how much would approach infinity. Installing closed-circuit cameras was an option but was unnecessary once our oldest turned eight: "Father, I have some information you might be interested in. It's about two boys whose names begin with 'J' and 'A.' Did you want a written report for your records?"

When we couldn't sort through dueling stories, all parties were held accountable. Of course, those more aggrieved—in their eyes—flung the "F" word: "fair." As in, "That's not fair."

Referring to the Parenting Manual, page 131, section C, my reflex response was "Life's not fair." After a few years, that started to sound pretty stale, so I substituted "You could be right."

Without any reason to bicker and battle, the kids were left with two options: (1) ignore one another—not realistic when roaming the same house; or (2) get along. By process of elimination, most choose number 2. Decrease the bad, and you automatically increase the good.

Randi held herself and the kids to the same standards. When feeling frustrated, before acting frustrated, she timed herself out in her room. Locking the door, she hung a sign, "Do not disturb," drew a bath, and soaked for an hour. I thought an hour time-out was excessive. She didn't. She didn't follow the "one minute per year of age in time-out" expert formula. She added as many minutes as she needed, leaving me all by myself to supervise. This parenting book is never going to get finished.

Lesson 14

Provide Backup

"If it were up to me, I'd let you do it." That may not rank as the dumbest thing I've ever said as a father, but it's up there. And it's definitely one of the dumbest things I've ever said as a husband.

Sammy, my eleven-year-old, had just sought my opinion shortly after his mother had given him hers. No surprise, but he couldn't keep my opinion between us. Half a nanosecond later, he found his mother, quoting to her my exact words, probably more than once to make sure she heard him right.

How was it that my children could forget something I had asked them to do just a minute earlier but could repeat word for word—months later—my gaffes? Then again, selective recall isn't unique to the young.

The next words I heard were my wife's: "Ray, you just threw me under the bus." Instead of suspecting that Sammy's recounting might be a bit slanted, I had impulsively opined. What's more, even were it accurate, so what? Mom had already delivered her decision.

Randi pointed out, quite legitimately, that (1) I had undermined her authority and (2) I had presented myself as the cooler, more reasonable parent, thereby making me look good and her look bad.

"Good cop, bad cop" is a common interrogation strategy. One detective of a pair assumes a softer demeanor, the other a more confrontational one. The contrast is intended to get someone to better cooperate.

Good cop, bad cop may be a savvy police move, but it's a foolish marital move. "Correcting" a spouse's discipline of a child in front of said child is courting marital discord. Should I think my wife's ruling questionable—which may mean not how I would have ruled—the time to talk is later. Most child-rearing split decisions don't need an immediate resolution. Wrangling over who's right and who's wrong, with a child listening nearby and taking notes, usually convinces only one person that she's right: the child.

Adults talk of the benefits of two good parents. They double the love, teaching, supervision, and support. Were we to ask the kids, we might hear a further plus: "Because if one says no, we can ask the other." Call it "appealing the decision."

Kids rival the skill of trial lawyers at overturning verdicts. Should Mason not get a full reversal, he can still seek a hung jury, which means terms remain open for negotiation.

My kids' standard appeal lines were: "Mom said it's okay with her if it's okay with you." "Mom didn't exactly say said no." "Mom wasn't sure about it, so I thought it'd be good to ask you." When all else fails, appeal to ego.

My defenses were honed with practice. "Are you sure that's exactly what Mom said?"

"Well, maybe not exactly."

"Let me see if Mom is really okay with this."

"That's okay, Dad, you don't need to. I'll check again."

"I'm going to check with Mom, and if what you're telling isn't completely true, you could be in some trouble."

"Now I remember, she also said . . ."

It's a miracle.

A successful appeal leads to "holding court." To illustrate, Mom is exasperated after a twenty-minute inquisition from thirteen-year-old Macy, who just cannot believe she isn't allowed to go to the mall with her new best friends—as of last week—Sybil and Snake. However well-stated Mom's reasons, Macy doesn't buy them.

Miffed by her mother's inflexibility, Macy dashes to Dad, enlightening him with her highly edited testimony. Dad listens, wanting to appear a fair-minded judge. "Why did Mom say you couldn't go? Who are Sybil and Snake? How long did you want to stay at the mall? Are you willing to check in with us every so often?"

Notice that Dad begins with "What did Mom say?" and ends with "Maybe we can work something out." Somewhere along the way, he moves from neutral party to advocate. Dad then approaches Mom, who is still steaming from Macy's "malling." Right behind him is Macy, eager to hear her case reopened.

"What's going on between you and Macy?" Definitely not a good opening for Dad. For one, his question is not really a question. It's a statement: "You two are at it again, I see." For another, Dad is looking to readjudicate. In effect, he is saying, "I'm here to find out who said what and why." Or worse, "I'm here to judge who is more at fault."

Mom feels double-teamed. Gamely, she explains herself. "I told Macy she is too young to go to the mall unsupervised. And that I have no idea who Sybil and Snake are. She kept arguing, got mouthy, saying 'Well, let's just see what Dad says,' and stormed out." Dad gives Macy a "You didn't tell me that part" look.

Sensing her case faltering, Macy launches, "Yesterday when I asked, she [note the "she," not "Mom"] said, 'I don't know. Dad and I might have to talk about it.' Then she just rules on her own and says no." On her own? That's a tattle: See, Dad, she doesn't even ask you what you think. She just goes and does it. Macy is mastering the divide and conquer.

To recover, Dad's best move would be to apologize to Mom for his hasty cross-examination. Alas, he forges ahead. "Macy is a good kid. Most of her friends go to the mall. It's not as if we can't trust her. Why don't we just call Snake's mom? What if Macy agrees to call us every so often?" Questions that all could be discussed privately but not publicly with Macy in the jury box.

Two verdicts here. Verdict 1: Mom's reasons needn't be acceptable to or understood by Macy. She has every right to make her ruling. Should only her gut tell her that Macy's mall cruise is a bad idea, her gut rules. Good parenting is saturated with good instincts.

Verdict 2: Even if Mom's style is not calm or cool, that is irrelevant. She has the authority to act in Macy's best interests. She can work on her style.

During marriage counseling, a spouse will protest the other's repeated taking him or her to child-rearing court. Rarely does it benefit either the parenting or the marriage. Rather, it incites feelings of betrayal.

Full disclosure: I have been pulled into court by a child a few times. I fell to the temptation to be mediator. After all, I am professionally trained.

Once, about thirty seconds into my opening remarks, Randi gave me "the look," as in, "Ray, what are you doing?" Simultaneously, my son gave me a look, as in, "Don't stop now, Dad. You're on a roll." Randi's look had much more stopping power.

An agreement that served us well: The parent who makes the rule rules. Meaning, the parent who sets the stronger standard—in media, peers, chores, respect, manners—sets the bar. One small example was Randi's rule: The younger children can't watch the Three Stooges. So, since her age ceiling was higher than mine,

I acquiesced and anticipated the day when my sons and I could take in Curly and the boys. At our inaugural viewing, we ate cake and ice cream.

Research confirms definite innate differences between boys and girls, men and women. As a father, I saw a lot of these differences, including one yet to be studied: Males dig the Three Stooges; women don't. An MIT nuclear-particle physicist, an orthopedic surgeon, and a psychologist all could watch the Stooges and, within minutes afterward, will "nyuk, nyuk" each other. Women, conversely, are of a unified impression: "They're not even funny; it's ridiculous." My sons flocked to the TV for the Stooges. My daughters and wife ignored them and us. Not once did any of my daughters "nyuk, nyuk" a sister.

When one of our children was having a bad day, marked by standing in the corner, sitting on the steps, or writing sentences, Randi would occasionally add an early bedtime. She said it was as much for her as for the child. Had I planned to take that child somewhere with me that evening, those plans were now suspended. Mom had supervised him all day; I didn't. The ruling was hers.

As our teens negotiated for more far-reaching freedoms, Randi, the at-home parent, had to apply the social brakes more often than did I. It was a practical matter. She was present, so she decided.

I offered a proposal: "Let me take the heat." Meaning, Randi could end any negotiation with, "Talk to your Dad. This is his idea." Hearing the first few times, "Mom says you're the one who decided this," I thought, "I did?" Then I remembered, "Yes, I did."

Parents don't always agree about what is best to do when and how. And more kids bring more opportunities to see things differently. So long as two big people with individual personalities are raising little people with individual personalities, that is unavoidable. It is wise to reach one mind later—on the couch, in bed, in the car, in a closet, wherever children don't roam. For Randi and me, some of the best meetings of our minds happened in solitude, in our bedroom, with chocolate-chip ice cream and hot fudge.

Lesson 15

Manners Matter

My grandfather, in his thick Italian accent, never missed reminding me whenever my boyhood self shuffled into his home, "Raymond, say 'hello' when you come in." No matter how low-profile my entrance, his voice found me. Likewise, upon leaving, "Always say, 'goodbye,' Raymond."

"Popo" landed at Ellis Island at age seventeen, speaking little English. When the immigration officer asked his name, he answered, "Quarante." The officer wrote down what he thought he heard—"Guarendi"—and with one stroke of a pen, from that day forward, it was our new family name.

Whether imported here from the "old country," as he called Italy, or adopted from his new country's ways, Popo expected manners. More than that, he insisted on them. It was the way he raised his sons, the way his son raised me, and the way I raised my children. Only one other parent in our home was more vigilant for good manners: the children's mother.

"How do you ask?" "What's the good word?" "Manners, please." "Say, 'excuse me.'" "What do you say when someone gives you something?" All these are standard manners mentoring. The prompting is reflexive. As my Latin teacher used to say, "Repetition for emphasis."

Speaking of repetition, my guesstimate is that before any of our children reached kindergarten, our courtesy coaching totaled hundreds, if not thousands, of times. An overstatement? Do the math: If we coached twice a day, in one year the tally would top seven hundred—for each child.

Why this emphasis on courtesy? Because courtesy is not merely rules of etiquette. It is much more. It communicates respect. It says, "I will treat you with social grace because I think you deserve it." Good manners speak well, not only of the one spoken to but also of the one speaking.

When out and about, if our kids spoke mannerly, accolades flowed their way. "What good manners!" "How polite!" "Isn't she sweet?"

The psychologist in me had to stifle an urge to respond. "Thank you, but don't put her sweetness to a vote from her siblings." The father in me couldn't help but preen a little.

Every so often, when it came time to pay our bill at a restaurant, we were informed, "It's been paid."

"By whom?" I asked.

"By a couple who was watching your family."

The statistician in me wanted to figure out just what they saw, so we could repeat it the next time out. Was it the crush of children at our table? The boys' ravenous eyeballing of their food, as though they hadn't eaten in days? My and Randi's keeping enough order to allow those within fifteen feet to eat in peace?

Rather than what they saw, was it what they heard? That is, at home or away, we prayed before meals. Occasionally, someone would stop by our table and comment favorably. Did they pick up our bill?

Then, too, it might have had something to do with our restaurant rule: When ordering, say "please"; when served, say "thank you"—without prompting. Risking no chance to go unheard above our table's dull roar, the children made sure to articulate their manners well above conversation level, sometimes obnoxiously so. Likely they were loud enough to be heard by every patron within a six-table radius and probably by some in the parking lot. Maybe one of them grabbed our tab. Manners pay.

Manners missed meant food dismissed. "When our server returns, you can try again." Which forced us to secure the unclaimed food from the vultures circling it. That I can recall, nobody ever lost a meal, though a few came within inches, only to be saved by a sibling's "What do you say?"—with the immediate addition: "If he forgets again, can I have it?"

People extrapolate from manners, rightly or wrongly, a host of admirable attributes: maturity, pleasantness, likability. And they reciprocate with smiles, accolades, and assorted goodies. "Such nice manners. Here are some cookies." Seeing it work so well for the kids, I tried it, echoing three or four times to a server, "Thank you." Never a cookie for me, though. How old is too old for manners rewards?

When a child was old enough to own his manners—usually between ages three and four—we decreed: To get something, say "please"; to keep it, say "thank you." To enter another's conversation, say "excuse me." These simple rules eliminated reminding while instilling manners better than any of our reiterating words could.

Teaching anything to kids doesn't as a rule advance in a straight line. More often, it is two steps forward, one step back, zigzagging its way to progress. For example, our younger ones presumed the go-ahead to interrupt any adult conversation with a rapid-fire string of "excuse me, excuse me, excuse me." In a no-word response to their "I want to talk right now," we held up a hand, silently saying, "Wait."

Should a child's "excuse me" fly right through our hand, the look on my face asked, "Are you forgetting something?" After child number four, it was a look that came more easily, not only with manners.

As kids—and parents—get older, monitoring manners can get sloppy. We figure, "Grace should have the idea by now. I don't need to be an echo chamber." With the years, a sort of social inertia sets in. Keeping courtesy to oneself becomes a habit. Many a fourteen-year-old isn't as polite as he was at five.

A core law of physics is the law of entropy. It states that over time everything decays—iron rusts, rocks crumble to dust, our bodies deteriorate. Sometime far into the future, the sun will burn out. The whole universe is winding down.

Relationships, too, can drift toward decay. Call it the law of social entropy. Compliments come fewer and farther between, affection cools, manners slip. If manners are a major good for my children, they are likewise a major good for me. Do I practice what I preach? Do I require from my kids what I don't require from myself? Are "please," "thank you," and "excuse me" basic to my own vocabulary, especially toward my spouse?

More than once—okay, lots more than once—a child corrected me, "Dad, is that how you ask?" I hate it when they bust me for ignoring my own rules. But I was not without defense, "No, it's not. And I'm glad you caught me, because I did that on purpose to see if you'd notice." Sure, Dad.

Lesson 16

We Raised People

It was our eldest's eighteenth birthday—his first day as a "legal" adult. The cake had been inhaled, the relatives had departed, and the last sibling had quit asking, "Did you get money in every card?" It was time for me to corner Andrew with my inaugural child-to-adult transition speech.

"Andrew, the law says you are now an adult. It seems like only yesterday you were a minor. At eighteen, you are free to no longer follow Mom's and my rules. You can come and go as you please, stay out late, eat whenever and whatever you want. Your freedoms have just exploded in the last twenty-four hours."

As my monologue inched toward a lecture—by Andrew's reckon, not mine—his kiddish grin got wider. He knew where I was headed.

"Yep, son, you can pretty much live your own way from here on out. Of course, if you do, you'll also have to live in your own place from here on out."

Andrew understood mathematics. Any minuses linked to our rules were more than offset by multiple plusses—free room and board, car access, insurance, technology, and sundry other household perks.

Kids play the numbers. It's called age entitlement. "I'm eighteen. I can do what I want now." "I'm sixteen. I can drive." "I'm twelve. I should have a smartphone." "I'm four. Where's my own bedroom?"

They've reached the milestone birthday, as so ordained by society, though not necessarily by Mom and Dad. In their minds, therefore, they merit a quantum leap in liberties. As I enlightened my first driving-age teen, "Sixteen is the minimum age at which the state says you are permitted to operate a vehicle. It's not the age we have to permit." Later teens heard the same. "I know, Dad."

A number is not a good guidepost for what freedoms to grant when. Trustworthiness is.

With both trustworthiness and maturity as our guides, we allowed licenses at different ages. Some kids drove shortly after reaching sixteen. Some not until eighteen. One showed little interest well into her twenties. As everyone's main driving instructor, I developed shin splints from repeatedly jamming my foot on the imaginary brake on my side of the car.

Linking age with license, or with any freedom, to juvenile eyes would appear more "fair." A number is fixed—much easier to measure than is "trustworthiness."

Freeman may announce, "As soon as I'm eighteen, the rules around here for me should change." Meaning, they should cease to rule me. He can believe so. A parent needn't.

What if the younger adult no longer wants to live under the older adult's rules? What if he thinks few, if any, apply to him anymore? What if he is older but no more mature? What if he's becoming more difficult to live with?

Exasperated parents ask me, "What can we do?" I reply, "You must decide that. It's your family, not mine." But in shrink-speak, I answer their question with my own questions. "Why are you allowing this ongoing lack of cooperation? When do you think things will improve? What is your limit? Do you have financial leverage? Are you willing to use that leverage to get better cooperation?"

A barrage of worries paralyzes parents into enduring a one-sided, freeloading relationship. How will he react if we set clear-cut conditions? How hard will he land if he's forced to move out? Could he fall in with a bad crowd? Drugs? Alcohol? Cohabitation? Will our relationship be forever ruined?

Anxious about any such outcomes, they endure almost daily turmoil, hoping that somehow, some way, someday, something will move this man-child (or woman-child) forward. Their head says, "Act." Their heart says, "Wait."

As a young father, I wondered what I would do in like circumstances. Could I stand strong? I thought so, but could I be certain? Any such day was years away. Would my resolve be shaken by emotion? How many second chances would I offer? At what point would I conclude that something had to change, and that I would have to be the one to change it?

Randi observed early in her motherhood, "To be a strong parent, I think you need a little bit of 'mean' in you." She didn't mean nastiness or harshness, but determination. She meant that a heart too soft could lead her to act in ways that would end up hurting the child she most wanted to help.

In an episode of the original *Star Trek* TV series, an evil force splits Captain Kirk into two persons. One is driven by feelings, hesitant to act for fear of error or upsetting someone. The other is a callous tyrant, ruling with a "Who cares how this affects you?" attitude.

No surprise, but the "soft" Kirk is too self-doubting to make the tough choices to benefit his crew, given any resistance. Only when both Kirks are reunited is he again a good leader, governed by truth and warmth.

Respect and cooperation: both were essential to live in our home post eighteen. Fortunately, for most of our children, this was not a problem. Not for all, though. One young adult, due to long-standing serious mental challenges, at age eighteen, under my court-appointed guardianship, entered a group home. Another, after a major incident following a trail of minor ones, was asked (not a request) to find other living arrangements.

Did this temporary turbulence badly bruise our relationship? Not for us. And for the most part, not for our children either. As they choppily navigated young adulthood, they more fully realized that Mom and Dad were less like the hard-hearted Captain Kirk and more like his blend.

Could a child ever return home? Yes, if facing a crisis or needing immediate help. Irresponsible living, however, would not be an acceptable reason to return. Again, our overriding question: "Will this help or hurt our son or daughter in the long run?"

My question as a young father had been answered. I could, with my wife beside me to stiffen my spine, muster the will to do what was needed — no, what was good — for them and for us.

The phrase "tough love" is an oxymoron. "Tough love" sounds contrary to "warm love" or "feeling love." Tough love is *love*, period. It is love motivating a parent to act in a child's best interests. It is love moved by faith and hope that someday she will be better understood and appreciated. Take it from a shrink father whose someday came: that does happen.

What if it doesn't? What if the twenties don't bring maturity? What if family friction lingers? What if immoral actions gain momentum?

Two answers:

1. Wisdom cannot always be judged by its outcome. Lacking Godlike vision, parents must routinely act upon

what they know when they know it. They choose their best—least bad?—options, knowing there will be unknowns.

2. The longer a conflict-laden living arrangement persists, the more ill will can fester. An ugly schism threatens, as all parties have "had enough." We fully meant to avoid that outcome.

A "minor" complication: Younger siblings may be watching and thinking, "Woah! Things change big-time when you're eighteen. One year, three months, nineteen days until I'm that age. Time then to party on."

As young adults leave home, many also leave the Faith. They suspect it, neglect it, or outright reject it. Throughout most of Christian history, what one was raised with, he pretty much stayed with. Not so much anymore. The surrounding society's morals—wrong word—do much to misshape minds and assault souls.

Parents come to my office confused and downcast. "We didn't raise him that way." And indeed they didn't. But they underestimated what did—the cultural and technological forces that surrounded and opposed them.

As our children moved into their twenties, the Faith of their family had to become their own. Some embraced it wholeheartedly. Some hugged select parts of it. A few drifted from it.

Why the disparate outcomes? All were raised by the same parents with the same beliefs in the same family. Yes, but none had the same personalities. They all heard the call of the culture differently. While Randi and I were a potent influence, we were not the sole one.

Many parents believe that a religiously wandering child harkens back to deficiencies in his child-rearing. To them, I present these yes-or-no questions:

Is there a God? Yes.

Is Christ God? Yes.

Was He sinless? Yes.

Could He perform miracles? Yes.

Did He have a perfect understanding of people? Yes.

Could He get most people to follow Him? (Pregnant pause) No.

Jesus Himself could not gather most as disciples. Was He lacking leadership skills? Did He not apply the right spiritual formulas? Did He need a better HR department?

You can't know when or if your child will return to the Faith of his youth. But the above logic should prove to you, as it did for me and Randi, that any religious self-blame needs to be over — permanently. Again, as my wife said, "We are not their Savior."

For decades, Randi and I were parents to little people. We remained parents, but those little people grew into big people, with their own choices, their own ways, their own lives — good or bad. Just like us.

Lesson 17

Know When to Wear Beige

Sit up, shut up, and wear beige advice given to mothers on a daughter's wedding day. Whimsical counsel with merit well beyond the wedding reception.

Watch, match, and wear wallet — my advice to fathers.

Our oldest married at age twenty-six. Along with the last-minute whirlwind of preps, plans, and place settings came ample openings to add our two cents' worth — two dollars' worth? "What if you tried this?" "Would another way work better?" Or the ever-dicey "Why are you doing it like that?" Two cents is worth most when wanted. Or when the wallet is handing it out.

Our philosophy: If asked, speak. If not, don't.

It is said: You never stop being a parent. If that means you never stop loving, giving affection, or showing concern, true. Few children, no matter how old, tire of these gifts.

Until my mother passed from this life, not two steps through her door, I heard, "Hi, honey. Are you hungry?"

"I'm good, Ma. I just ate."

"How about a sandwich?"

"No thanks. I'm full."

"Did you want some fruit? A piece of cake? There's chicken in the refrigerator."

I had to resurrect a dietary strategy I mastered as a child at my food-filled Italian grandmother's house: Say yes to the first offered menu item, then nurse it for the whole visit. Every few bites or so, Grandma asked, "Is that all you're going to eat?"

As I left Mom's, I heard, "Is your coat warm enough? Do you need another pair of gloves? It's barely fifty degrees outside." Some big boys might be miffed by this "You're still my little boy." I wasn't. My mother was showing her love for her son, no matter his age. Besides, sometimes I was really hungry.

"Hey, Dad, what do you think about ...?" "What did you do, Mom, when we ...?" "Can you check my car? There's a weird squeak coming from somewhere in the engine."

As our children moved toward more independence, we had to move toward more mouth control, asking ourselves, "Do they want our input?" If it sounded so, we were happy to give it. I took longer than Randi to learn to measure my words. You never stop being a parent.

Is my advice—in case you want it—never to say one word about how a young adult is living, especially when poorly? No. What you instilled all those years may once again need a booster. The key phrase is "once again." When "once again" becomes "again and again," the chance for discord or an all-out breach rises. When "I'm your parent. I know better, and I'll keep telling you that" keeps intruding into conversations, the risk is that communication overall shuts down.

When the urge to speak up overwhelms, follow the discipline dictum, K.I.S.S.—keep it short and simple. Overtalking overlong is asking for closed ears, glazed eyes, or "back off" comebacks. Probing endlessly for the perfect logic to make oneself better heard may make one less heard.

"I know, Dad." This can mean "I agree." Or "You've told me this before." Or "I know that's how you see it, but I don't." Or "I really don't want to hear this." How I understood "I know" told me whether to say more, say less, or say nothing.

The transition from years of everyday guidance to prudent reticence is neither easy nor smooth. Most parents—me included—can't flip an off switch, in essence washing our hands: "You're raised. Whatever you do from here on is your business." Nor would most parents want to. Still, however slow and hesitant the transition, wisdom may dictate moving toward fewer words, not more.

Lectures track a predictable course. Parent begins talking; child begins listening; parent talks more; child listens less; parent persists; child sleeps with eyes open. The whole exchange (a misnomer) advances (another misnomer) at one moment in time and space. However well stated—at the risk of repeating myself—lectures follow the law of diminishing returns: the longer, the less absorbed.

All lectures don't start and stop in one sitting, however. Some revisit the same topic over weeks, months, possibly years. In effect, they become one reiterating lecture with intermittent breathers.

My wife listened longer sooner than I did. In my defense, I had to overcome years of an education touting overtalking. Recalling the lyrics of "The Gambler" helped: "You've got to know when to hold 'em." Sound advice not only for cards but for words.

No question, witnessing a young adult get schooled by reality is hard on a parent's heart. Why can't he just listen? It would save him lots of bumps and bruises. Why is he making the world teach him?

As life continues to speak with the same voice as Mom and Dad, though, a young person may find some credence in the folks' wisdom. To paraphrase Mark Twain: "When I was eighteen, my father knew next to nothing. By the time I was twenty-one, I was shocked by how much smarter he had become." Sadly, some young people need more than three years to arrive at a Twain-like epiphany.

Taught by Ten

Watching a young person live poorly—socially, emotionally, morally—can compel a parent to keep trying to "fix it." It's her duty, as she sees it. Somehow, some way, she must reach this errant young person. Then, too, she is often haunted by the question, "How much of this is my fault?"

However well meant, continuing to preach after meeting "Stop the preaching" doesn't persuade; it dissuades. It irritates. The morally adrift youngster knows full well what her parents believe. She grew up with it. Her choices now don't reflect a lack of knowledge. They reflect, for the time being anyway, a willful turnabout.

Relationships take on an edginess when a touchy subject lurks around the next sentence. Saying less about someone's conduct does not at all mean you condone it. Should a young person open the door to talking, walk gently through it. Otherwise, knock repeatedly when there is no answer, and soon the door may be locked.

St. Ambrose, bishop of Milan, spoke very wise words to St. Monica, a mother deeply distressed over her wayward, God-ignoring son Augustine—that same Augustine who, years later, converted and is now known as St. Augustine, one of the Catholic Church's foremost teachers. St. Ambrose said, "Talk less to your son about God, and more to God about your son."

It's said: "A smart person learns from his mistakes. A smarter person learns from the mistakes of others." I might add: "A smart young person learns from smarter older persons. And a smarter older person learns when to be quiet."

Beige is fast becoming my color.

Lesson 18

We Already Raised Our Children

"You need to finish your ice cream before I give you another cookie." "You can stay up a little longer, but only until midnight. Then it's to bed, okay?" "I promise—this is the last stuffed animal I'll buy her this week." "She didn't mean to push him down all three times. She's just tired."

So speaks the stereotype of the soft, goodie-giving grandparent, those whose child-rearing practices are a fading echo of their younger years. Quipped one comedian, "These are not the same people who raised us. Some aliens took over their bodies." Or, as enthused one grandmother, "If I had known grandkids were so much fun, I'd have had them first."

The softy stereotype is showing cracks, however. More grandparents are perplexed at their children's raising their kids with a looseness they never saw when they themselves were raised. In many ways, these parents look more like grandparents than do the grandparents.

My days of being a young parent are long past. Truth be told, this is as old as I've ever been. Given so, I've been around long enough to observe firsthand some clear generational shifts. There is less "I'm the parent; you're not" and more "Is this the way you want it, Bliss?" Out with parental authority, in with democratic negotiation.

The upshot: More grandparents are slower to "spoil" their grandkids and quicker to correct their parents. They're hesitant to indulge a child whom they see as already indulged, and they feel the urge to comment on the parent's permissiveness. They may want to be the loosey-goosey grandparent, but they aren't sure that role is open to them.

Randi and I have five grandchildren. From the first wail of our first grandchild, we've been itching to consult—pro bono. After all, between the two of us, we've tallied 360-plus years of practice. We are willing to donate a few years' worth.

We're willing but waiting. Until, that is, we are given some subtle invite like "Help! What do I do with her now?"

Sounds odd, doesn't it? Reticence like this coming from someone who makes a living dispensing advice. Yes, but most are seeking that advice. Some even pay me for it. Still, at home or away, my general counsel is: Don't counsel those who don't ask or don't want.

"Not all who don't ask, don't want." True, but reading who wants and when is not so easy. What's more, someone can want but, upon receiving, change his mind. The safer course is to wait for the opening. Timing is a key to helpfulness.

"Dad, can I ask you a question?" So began a phone call from my son. The question was not about his yard, his car, enamel versus water-based paint, or whether the DH in baseball is good for the game. No, it was about his two-year-old daughter, Rose. I asked back, "Are you asking me for kid advice?" "Yes." "Can you put that in writing?" After wiping a tear of gratitude, I gave Andrew my ideas, along with an offer to sell him one of my parenting books—for half price. He is my son.

Grandparent guidance comes in three Cs.

Comment. "She has a mind of her own, doesn't she?" "He gets feisty when he doesn't get his way." Are these comments about the child, as in, "He's his own person, isn't he?" or about the parent, as in, "Shouldn't you be stronger?"

While remarks like these may sound fairly benign, too many given too freely can be misheard. "Limited" is the rule of thumb, or as it were, rule of mouth.

Correction. "Wouldn't it be better just to ignore that behavior?" "You need to pick your battles." Corrections carry the tone: "I know better. As you know, I did raise children for a long time." The question is not "Do you know better?" You may well. The question is, "Are these your children?"

Our grandchildren are first and foremost our children's children. Do Randi and I have more child-rearing know-how? Measured by the number of kids and years, yes, no matter how many books our children might read (not usually mine). Even so, our turn at child-rearing is over. It is now our children's turn. They have the right to make decisions for their families, however we might view those decisions.

Critique. "Why would you do it that way? You're just making it worse." "No wonder she gets so mad. Look at how you deal with her."

Critiques shout: "You're a bad parent!" Even if accurate, they won't win an ear or change a mind. "Thank you for helping me take a hard look at my shortcomings. Once I can get past the sting of your words, I will see their truth." Only the most self-assured parent can accept criticism wrapped around a put-down.

Critiques assail a parent's sense of competence—even being heard as questioning her love for her children. Definitely, they hold the most potential to batter or shatter a relationship.

"I'm only trying to help." Likely so. Most grandparents don't intend to diminish or disparage their children's ways. They intend to instruct. Again, that may not be how they're heard. When the signs are coming fast that what is meant as help isn't being received as help, it's time to stop helping—fast.

One subject where we don't always wait for an invite concerns faith and morals. All our children know what we believe. They've had years of living with it. Typically, though, we rely on openings to present themselves. If they do, we don't nag or belabor. There comes a point where "enough said" is plenty said.

When the relationship with a son, daughter, or in-law breaks, all too often the three Cs have built toward a critical mass. Sadly, one result is that the grandparents are allowed little or no contact with the grandchildren. Sadder still, religious differences underlie many a severed relationship. It could have been avoided, or at least eased, by easing up on comments about the parents' religious ways or lack thereof.

Slow to speak doesn't always mean slow to act. Suppose Buck is yanking Mom or Dad around—in words or conduct. Either oblivious or bickering with him, they don't look my way for help. Therefore, I merely watch. I have suggestions, but I keep them to myself. If the action gets heated enough, I might hear, "Dad, you got any ideas here?" Glad you asked.

What if I am Buck's target? When Mom or Dad is present, the correction is first theirs, not mine. Should they do nothing, then I will act.

I can defend myself, but can my house defend itself? It's a silent bystander, helpless against a child's misdirected meanderings. If no other big person is moving to protect it, I will.

When my kid-roaming instincts pushed me to explore my grandmother's bedrooms or workroom, she intervened. "Raymond, stay out of there." If my folks didn't do anything, she did. If my mother was preoccupied or my father was asleep, I made my move. My grandmother, I was convinced, never slept.

One grandparent told her son, as his little Petunia was stomping toward her flowerbeds, "How she treats your flowers is up to you. How she treats mine is up to me." Is that a comment or a correction? Sometimes they overlap.

A big no-no for us is overruling or undercutting our children's decisions. If Mom doesn't allow Oscar to watch *The Tomato That Burped Up Chicago*, we don't either when he's with us, no matter how cute or harmless we think the movie. When Dad sends daughter to the corner, never do we rescue her from "mean old Dad," freeing her from his "unfair" incarceration. That is not our place.

Another no-no is compensation, that is, giving a grandchild perks, gifts, and goodies to offset the parents' "too strict" or "unreasonable" childrearing. A direct relationship: Compensation, overt or sneaky, risks more limits on contacts.

Our grandchildren's parents have the right to be more loose than we would be. So, too, do they have the right to be more tight than we would be.

Some parents are very open to grandparents' guidance, some not so much, and some not at all. Learning quickly which is which can go far to keep the grandparent-parent-grandchild connection solid.

And with the birth of each grandchild, Randi bought me another pair of beige pants.

Lesson 19

Don't Blink

Que sera, sera.

"Would you want to know your future?" My first impulse would be an emphatic "No! Absolutely not!" The mind can concoct no end of "What ifs"—many, if not most, of which never will happen—to keep it perpetually unsettled. Adding "Definites" to "What ifs" is a merger that leaves little peace in the present.

The actress Doris Day made famous the song "Que Sera, Sera."

> When I was just a little girl,
> I asked my mother,
> "What will I be?" ...
> Here's what she said to me:
> "*Que, sera, sera.*
> Whatever will be, will be.
> The future's not ours to see.
> *Que sera, sera.*"[4]

Under one condition, however, would I answer, "Yes, I want to see the future." That is, to know what present-day negatives

[4] Jay Livingston and Ray Evans, "Que Sera, Sera" (1955).

123

would become one-day positives, which misfortunes would come to be fortunes.

As a yet-to-be father, I looked forward to the birth of my children. When my body said, "That's not going to happen," my mind said, "That's a biological smack in the face."

It is said, "We don't know what we don't know." To which could be added: "We don't know what we will know." Randi and I were left with a "What now?" God knew what now. Looking back, I can imagine Him saying, "Be patient. Let me work on this."

As our children grew from infants to teens to adults to parents themselves, what we saw as hurts and troubles became benefits and blessings. Which ones we couldn't predict. We found out, though, and we wait upon whatever good may still come. The word for it is "hope."

Psychological Correctness

There are no foolproof formulas for raising kids. Formulas inhabit the worlds of math and chemistry. Parenthood is too fluid and flexible—and long—for formulas. Rather, some ways work better and some worse. You decide which work best for you, based upon your personality, your child's personality, and your convictions. An expert's prescription may get you where he thinks you should go, not necessarily where you want to go.

As a psychologist, I'm familiar with many of the "psychologically correct" ways to talk, to listen, to discipline (or not)—in short, to raise children expertly. As a father, I found some helpful, some useless, and some downright dopey. Some sounded good on paper, but they failed with real kids.

Did my professional experience help me raise my own children? Yes, but not so much because I knew all the "cutting edge" stuff. More so, it was because I learned better who kids are, what to expect from them, and why they don't always understand or agree with me.

Along the way, I knew I'd make my share of honest mistakes. And I knew I'd have my share of opportunities to look back—whether an hour later or a year—realizing, "I could have handled that better." Such is the nature of being all too human.

What's more, I knew that fearing miscalculations or missteps would erode, paralyze even, my willingness to take the strong stances crucial to my children's well-being. And when my stances went against those of the culture, I knew to brace myself, as I would be challenged not only by my children—that's natural—but by other parents and society. So be it.

In the end, if any of my children veered from how they were raised, I wanted to know it was because they had to get past me and not because I stepped aside.

Butch and Felicity

Some children raise their parents to believe they're God's gift to parenthood. Others syphon off an average of six IQ points per year. "When my first child was a toddler, I refused to hang my knickknacks suspended in cages from the ceiling. Butch knew that my no meant no. Then Felicity came along, and I can't prove it, but I think she sold two of my knickknacks and ate a third."

All children, even identical twins, have their own unique temperaments. Every parent knows this or is forced to face it as each temperament asserts itself all along the way.

Our children were a medley of diverse personalities. Some readily embraced our teaching, or most of it anyway. A few had to find out for themselves, one shaky step at a time, that we knew something about life. And a few always seemed to be asking, "What are you trying to tell me?"

Suppose a 1-to-10 child-rearing scale, with 1 being the child who, by age three, can pretty much run the house and 10 being a tad less tough than training a Grizzly. A minority are 1s and 2s and 8s and 9s, with most falling in the 4–6 range.

Acknowledging this scale helped us to stride through parenthood more comfortably. We stressed less with the tougher kids and laughed more with all of them. As my wife reminded me often, "We are raising people." True enough—each with his own inborn personality interacting with ours.

Good Authority, Less Discipline

Child-rearing gurus have demeaned authority. To many, it's an archaic leftover from less-educated parenting days. If asserted, it is to be asserted sparingly, as a last resort. Other less "controlling" substitutes will prompt more willing cooperation while eliminating much discipline. Or so they contend.

"How do you do it? I'm overloaded with my two," parents would ask Randi 'long about our fourth child.

One answer: Authority. Randi established hers early. It was not an autocratic "Don't think to question me." Rather, it was clear expectations backed by meaningful consequences. Authority doesn't make only a parent's life smoother. It makes everyone's life smoother, in multiple ways.

1. Authority eases friction. It lessens arguments, hot emotions, and discipline clashes. Troublesome times came fewer and farther between.

2. Authority is clear and present. When a child knows a parent will act if need be, the less the parent will have to act. Authority doesn't lead to more discipline; it leads to less.

3. Authority makes reason more persuasive. Words are better heard when authority backs them.
4. Authority reduces the agitation that can breed harsh words and overreaction. It speaks softly but strongly. It is loving.

Lots of benefits coming from an old-fashioned, expert-snubbed word.

Affection: Countering the Culture

As a parent details for me a long list of his teen's unruly behaviors, he often adds, "I think I'm giving you the wrong impression. Overall, he's a pretty good kid." Asking for elaboration, I hear, "Well, he's not on drugs or anything like that." As long as Conan is getting decent grades, is avoiding legal trouble, and isn't uncontrollable, he's a "pretty good kid." The culture's moral high bars are dropping.

Raising a civilized child is much easier than raising a virtuous child. The latter takes more authority, vigilance, and persistence. It also takes more affection, given freely and regularly.

The culture convinces youth, "Your parents are so stuck in yesterday, refusing to move into today."

When your standards are well above society's, love must speak loudly. And little speaks love more loudly than affection. Everyday, wholehearted expressions of affection will draw a youngster closer to your ways than to society's ways.

Make Her Be Different

"How can I be different from how I am?" In so many words, the question those in counseling ask. Even among the most motivated, however, personal growth can be a "two steps forward, one step backward" trek, involving time and effort—lots.

"How can I make someone else be different from how he is?" That is the much harder question to answer. When one is captain of his own ship, steering it is tough enough. When not the captain of another's ship, steering it is that much tougher, if it can be done at all.

If my grown child is acting in ways that are self-defeating, morally misguided, or just plain dumb, I feel compelled to speak up, to steer him in the right direction. As a good parent, should I not do so, however long it takes?

Well, yes and no. (Don't you just love shrinks?) Yes, in that, if my guidance is welcomed, I'll feel better, and my son or daughter will do better. It's a win-win. No, in that if it is ignored or rejected, then I had best shut up. Pushing, prodding, or preaching risks straining or potentially fracturing our relationship.

All of our children are in their twenties and thirties. As they've moved into adulthood, we—I more than Randi—have had to navigate a learning curve, that is, to learn better when to speak to whom about what. No longer was I Dad guiding my young children day to day. I was now Dad relating to young adults, with their own individual lives. Sure, I think I have good things to say. The question is: How receptive is my audience?

Being a parent to a grown-up is very different from being a parent to a child.

A smart parent knows what to say. A wise parent knows whether to say it.

Don't Blink!

Is this the little girl I carried?
Is this the little boy at play?
I don't remember growing older. When did they?
When did she get to be a beauty?

Don't Blink

When did he grow to be so tall?
Wasn't it yesterday when they were small?[5]

Lyrics to "Sunrise, Sunset" from the play *Fiddler on the Roof*, as a
father and mother look back on their all-too-fleeting days as parents.
The country ballad "Don't Blink" sings of the same theme:

Don't blink, 'cause just like that you're six years old
And you take a nap
And you wake up and you're twenty-five
And your high school sweetheart becomes your wife

Don't blink, you just might miss
Your babies growing like mine did
Turning into moms and dads....

So don't blink....

I was glued to my TV, when it looked
Like he looked at me and said
"Best start putting first things first"

'Cause when your hourglass runs out of sand
You can't flip it over and start again
Take every breathe God gives you for what it's worth....
Don't blink.[6]

Just last month, my wife and I trooped into church with ten
kids under age twelve. A week later, nine cars were parked in our
driveway, as several teens had licenses. A week after that, only two

---

[5] Jerry Bock and Sheldon Harnick, "Sunrise, Sunset," *Fiddler on the Roof* (1964).
[6] Kenny Chesney, "Don't Blink," *Just Who I Am: Poets & Pirates* (BNA Records, 2007).

kids were living at home. Yesterday, Randi and I sipped morning coffee in the kitchen, looking at grandkids' pictures on our phones.

"Do you have any regrets?" Answering my friend's query again, I'd say, "I regret when I didn't fully relish the everyday with my children — more snuggling at bedtime, playing longer kickball games, running beside — behind? — them from house to house on Halloween to swell our candy haul, looking up more often from my writing just to watch them play."

If I could flip the hourglass over, I'd put more of me into the all-too-fleeting moments of parenthood. My priorities would better assume their proper places — God first, family second, me third — the absolute right order for being a better husband and father. And one my children are still teaching me. Don't blink.

About the Author

Dr. Ray Guarendi is a Catholic husband, the father of ten adopted children, a clinical psychologist, an author, a professional speaker, and an international radio and television host. His radio show, *The Doctor Is In*, can be heard on the EWTN Global Catholic Radio Network on SIRIUS/XM, iHeart Radio, and more than 500 domestic and international AM & FM radio affiliates. His TV show, *Living Right with Dr. Ray*, can be seen on EWTN and reaches more than 380 million homes in 145 countries and territories.